THE ABORTIONIST'S SON

BY

DAVID DAVIS

WHAT WOULD YOU DO IF...

Table of Contents

THE
PHOENIX
ORGANIZATION

Thank you for your support of the Author's rights
and The WDavis Foundation.
For additional information please go to the website:
www.theabortionistsson.com

or

www.Wdavisfoundation.com

This book is a combination of facts about David Davis's life and certain embellishments. Names, dates, places, events, and details have been changed, invented, and altered for literary effect. The reader should not consider this book anything other than a work of literature.
1st edition published 2016 by The Phoenix Organization.
ISBN: 978-0-578-18196-7
Book and cover design by Vashti Harrison

AUTHOR'S NOTE

At its heart, this book has several messages I want to pass on to people. The idea of loyalty to family is such a powerful one, reinforced at every turn. Unfortunately, that idea was used to manipulate and control me; my longing to be loved, to belong, to be a loyal son made me willing to do things I deeply regret.

My story is a cautionary tale, one that if read carefully will prevent you from making the same mistakes that I did while trying to protect my family. If you remove the element of family from the story, I would have never helped Johnny Russell do the things he did. It is something that I now have to live with for the rest of my life.

A lot of comments will be made about the reason I wrote this book. To be completely honest, there is more than one reason, but if just one person can benefit from the lessons I learned and not go through the pain and suffering I experienced, then this book was worth writing. The event that pushed me from thinking about writing this book to doing it was the day I found out I was going to be an uncle.

From that moment on, I was going to protect my nephew from Johnny Russell, no matter what the personal cost to me. I started to write my story. After finishing the book and witnessing the extent of the denial and enabling within my family, I had no choice but to publish it.

This is a story of greed, excess, guilt and betrayal on an unprecedented level. I make no excuses for my actions and I will have to pay for what I have done for the rest of my life. I get down on my knees everyday and pray for forgiveness for my part in things with Johnny. It took dying twice and being in a coma for 20 days to truly realize the mistakes I made.

My hope in writing this book is that people realize that there are a lot of Johnny Russell's in this world and if you trust them, you could pay the same price I did. The sad truth is we live in a world that contains both good people and bad, some are saints and some are monsters; inevitably, some of them are family.

THE ABORTIONIST'S SON

CHAPTER ONE

VEGAS

To say, I hate Las Vegas is an understatement.

Even before any of this happened, it always felt like people there were trying too hard. Of course, Johnny loves Vegas because no one judges you as long as your wallet is full. He loves the fact that his money makes him a god there.

It is this fact and my increasingly guilty conscience that are giving me second thoughts about the trip we are about to take. What started out as doing the right thing in my mind has mutated into something else entirely.

The week before our trip, I finally called Johnny and told him I didn't want to be involved with the details anymore. He had asked me to do him a favor and handle booking his girlfriend's plane ticket, and I had reluctantly agreed to help him. Even though he wired me the money and it wasn't my money paying for the ticket, this act had really bothered me.

It was as if I had switched from watching his back to participating and it was a line I wasn't willing to cross again.

The call goes well and to my surprise, he says, "No problem, I will handle everything after this trip."

Encouraged by his response, I lay down the ground rules for this trip. One, whatever he does is his business; I don't want to be involved with it anymore or have any knowledge of it. Two, I get a room of my own, so I don't have to be involved with whatever he has planned for this weekend. Finally, I will cover for him as long as he obeys my simple requests, but I am only *covering* for him, not participating. This is *his* thing. He agrees to my requests a little too quickly, but I hope that's an indication that he now realizes how uncomfortable I am with the whole thing.

The thought of this "vacation" has haunted me since I booked it. I wake up Friday morning exhausted by the idea of what lies ahead and I try and psyche myself up. *It is just a long weekend,* I keep telling myself on the way to the airport.

On the flight to Vegas, I switch from the "dreading-it" phase to the "just get through it" portion of the "Johnny Russell Experience." As I order my second Bloody Mary, I start to question whether I am overreacting to being sucked into the whole thing. *Man up*, I keep telling myself, but deep down I know this is just wrong.

He doesn't call it the "Johnny Russell Experience" and would be furious if he found out I came up with a term to describe what he does. It is a way for me to detach myself from the whole thing. *I am a beard and nothing more*, I keep reminding myself as the plane starts its descent. The truth is it took me a while to even figure out the real purpose of these trips. In the beginning, I was so out of my depth with Johnny that it took me some time to just process what he was doing.

While I am the opposite of a prude, there are certain lines I never crossed until I met Johnny. He talks about it like it is just a male bonding thing and a way to blow off some steam. I honestly don't know what to call it, but it is the opposite of a good time as far as I am concerned. Unfortunately, he seems dead set on sharing this experience with me and this thought turns my stomach a little. As the wheels touch the ground, I am hit with a new concern, *what if he tries to surprise me with someone on this trip?*

Las Vegas, Nevada: May 12th, 2011

As soon as I get off the plane, I am immediately met by Johnny and his new girlfriend, Cindy. She looks like she is in her late twenties with long brunette hair and I hear her thick New York accent as she says, "Nice to meet you. Are you psyched for this weekend or what?"

I smile at her while I shake her hand and lie with a simple, "Can't wait."

This response elicits a big smile from Johnny as he takes over and starts giving orders. "Let's get your luggage and find a cab to take us to the hotel."

I look over at Cindy as we walk to baggage claim. I am not the only person to go through the "Johnny Russell Experience," and while I know what is coming, this girl has no clue. I feel a slight twinge of guilt as we pick up my bags and walk through the baggage claim exit.

Of course, as with anything that involves Johnny, things don't go as planned. Cindy informs us she couldn't find a friend for me to bring along for the trip as we walk to the cab.

That's why he agreed to my condition so quickly, I realize feeling both relief and disappointment, *he was just going to surprise me with her friend.*

As I am thanking God for my good fortune in dodging that bullet, Cindy volunteers to sit in the front seat with the cab driver, giving Johnny and me a chance to talk.

"Do you want to split her with me?" Johnny asks me as soon as the cab leaves the airport curb.

Split her with him? I think to myself, as I try my best to hide my shock and disgust at the idea.

"No thanks, she's all yours," I say quickly and then turn to look out the window as the cab heads toward downtown Vegas navigating through the afternoon traffic.

The same question keeps repeating over and over in my mind, *why me?*

Before this trip, I spent a lot of time thinking about how I was going to separate myself from Johnny's idea of a "good time." That's why I insisted on separate rooms. I love women, but not when they are paid for, and I won't cross that line again. In seeing how Johnny operated on the first couple of trips, I wanted to minimize my exposure to the whole thing.

I turn my thoughts to what comes next and try to erase the question Johnny just asked me from my brain. I try and look at the bright side. Now that his plan to surprise me with someone has backfired, I realize I am completely off the hook. For a moment, I allow myself to relax and just take in the sights.

Maybe this won't be so bad after all, I think to myself as a miniature version of New York passes by my side of the cab.

This is when we run into problem number two. Johnny's new girlfriend is a smoker. And Johnny hates smokers. At this point, I am trying not to laugh as I wonder, *Maybe karma really does exist?* This is a man who asks the waiter to change seats if a diner who just *smelled* of smoke sat next to him. Now he has a weekend "girlfriend" who doubles as a human chimney stack!

Of course, this momentary setback doesn't deter Johnny from starting to turn on the charm in the cab as he starts the process of "winning" Cindy over. Each attempt Johnny makes at being charming is cringe worthy, and I absently wonder what the cab driver is thinking.

Johnny's lines and plays are so predictable and lame that you almost feel sorry for him. Of course, the cab driver doesn't know this is his strategy. He wants the girls to feel as if this is his first time and that he is really trying. Everyone gets to play a different part in the "experience," and I feel sorry for Cindy because she doesn't even know she is playing her part yet.

The truth is that Johnny wants these women to love him, *no joke!* He wants them to connect on an emotional level and goes to great lengths to make that happen.

We pull up to one of the nicer hotels in Vegas and take the elevator to get to the hotel lobby. This is when Cindy informs Johnny of problem number three. It's that time of the month for her. As the door opens, I am having a hard time keeping a straight face.

Maybe I will get to enjoy this trip a little? I think to myself, as I start to smile a little.

As we walk out into the hotel lobby, Johnny asks me if he could speak to me in private for a moment. We excuse ourselves and leave Cindy with our bags by a couch next to the check in counter.

My momentary happiness immediately disappears, as soon as I see the cold rage in his eyes. Johnny has now realized that his carefully arranged plans have turned to shit, and it looks like he is about to explode.

"What's up?" I ask him trying to play dumb, not wanting to add fuel to the fire.

"Soon should have known better than to send me a smoker who is on her period. I'll make sure she pays for this!" Johnny hisses in a quietly furious tone.

I have heard this tone before, and my blood pressure starts to kick up a notch. Johnny's mood swings can turn dark very quickly, and I don't want him causing a scene in the hotel lobby. This has the potential to go bad in an instant, and I can't risk that happening. The rooms are in my name, so I try to calm him down by breaking one of my ground rules.

"Relax. Cindy can sleep in my room if the smoker thing bothers you that much." I tell him calmly, but he looks far from happy as he continues to glare over at her. I try to put out the fire by getting her out of his line of sight.

"Why don't you go to your room and unpack," I suggest calmly as I try and diffuse the situation. "She can stay in my room while you get comfortable and I will talk to her about the cigarettes. Let's just try and make the best of it."

He pauses for a moment to think things through before saying, "Fine, just handle it." With that, he marches to the check in counter leaving me to inform Cindy of the new sleeping arrangements.

Once Cindy and I get to my room, I make it crystal clear that she is off the clock. I already feel pretty bad for her because when Johnny isn't happy with someone, he really knows how to make him or her feel like absolute shit. I think she realizes I am only trying to make the best out of an already awkward situation, and she relaxes a little. After about thirty minutes of watching TV together, she excuses herself to start getting ready for our first night out on the town.

As the sun starts to set, Johnny knocks on my door, and he's in good spirits. I desperately hope that whatever prescription cocktail he's on will last the entire evening and the Johnny I can't stand doesn't make a return appearance. Every trip, it feels like I am walking on eggshells when I am around him. There is no way to predict which version of Johnny I am going to get.

Luckily, there are no explosions, and everything goes off like clockwork. We have a nice dinner followed by catching The Elvis Show. After the show, we immediately head back to the hotel, and I am looking forward to a little time alone.

During the cab ride back, Johnny and Cindy start making out in the backseat. In anticipation of this happening, I volunteered to sit up front with the cab driver. My conversation with our driver gives me a chance to distract myself from what is going on in the back, and I am thankful it is only a five-minute ride back to the hotel.

Once we arrive at the hotel, Cindy and Johnny race to his room, and I collapse on the bed in mine. I relax for the first time since I woke up this morning. I try to stay positive and tell myself, "Relax, you just cleared the first hurdle, only two more days to go!"

As I lie on my bed, I start to think about everything that has happened since I met Johnny Russell. By now, being involved in his sordid double life is beginning to grind me down. There are times that I don't think I can keep it up. His threats, his erratic behavior, his mood swings and the sheer number of lies I have to keep up with are becoming too much for me, not to mention seeing the "girlfriends" go through the cruelty of the "experience."

Even though everyone is doing things of their own free will, seeing him play this game with women is starting to weigh heavily on me. I find it harder and harder to look myself in the mirror when I shave in the morning, and I haven't had a good night's sleep since this started.

"How do I get out of this mess?" I ask myself softly for the thousandth time.

At first, I just wanted to protect Johnny and try to figure out what was wrong with him. Unfortunately, the more I find out about him, the less I want to know. I take a big pull from my drink and try not to think about it anymore.

After a couple of hours of quality time, Cindy comes back to my room. I am still lying on the bed dressed in a t-shirt and sweats. I immediately remind her again that she is in a safe environment. As I've said, I love women, but there are certain lines I will never cross. I'm already feeling sorry for Cindy, as I see that she is starting to buy Johnny's act.

She starts to tell me about her experience so far with Johnny.

It always starts out the same: he wants to get to know them and makes really embarrassing attempts to win them over. These cheesy attempts somehow come off as sincere. He has been doing this for a very long time and knows just how far to push without going too far, but the result is always the same. They slowly start to open themselves up to him as he starts to share about his life.

The life of Johnny Russell reads like the human version of *Old Yeller*. He tells them that he has devoted his life to saving the unborn children in war-torn Afghanistan, even risking his life to do so. He paints himself as a selfless doctor-hero who is just looking for a girlfriend to love.

The women fall for it every time. I wouldn't mind so much, but I know how this tale ends.

The next morning, Cindy is in a great mood and looking forward to the day. She sings in the bathroom (and her voice isn't half bad). I am happy she is happy, but my mood is tempered by the knowledge of what is to come. There is nothing I can do at this point; she has already taken the bait.

We all want to believe that there is someone special out there for us. I can tell Cindy is starting to believe that Johnny is the one: he's kind, well-off and into her. Most prostitutes know better, but Johnny has a knack for finding the ones that are looking for a better life, looking for a way out.

The phone rings. It's for Cindy. "Your brother wants me to come to his room for a second, I will be right back!" she says as she happily skips

out the door. I immediately turn on the TV and find a pay per view movie; I know this is going to take a while. Three hours later, Cindy is back
with the glow of someone who is falling in love. We start to get ready to
lay out at the pool when Cindy asks me sweetly, "Can you give me the
bathroom for a minute? I need to douche out my ass."

Okay. No problem. I think as I walk into my room and head butt the
wall. *Why me?! What did I do to deserve this?!!*

Johnny knocks on the door, grinning from ear to ear. He is the post-
card picture of happy Johnny – charming, your best friend, a lot of fun
to be around.

The only problem is you never know when the other Johnny's are
going to make an appearance.

He insists we all wear sunscreen since "the sun is the enemy!" As I
am putting it on, I keep wondering, *how someone so morally bent can be
worried about skin cancer*?

Then I remember that we are still in the "honeymoon" phase of the
"experience." This is all part of the act. He wants to come across as the
good Johnny, the one that really cares, but has never found the right person to build a life with. I am part of the act to him, a prop if you will.

As I put on the sunscreen, I start counting down the hours until I am
back on the plane to LA. I keep telling myself this will be over soon and I
wonder if Cindy is thinking the same thing when I look over at her. *Nope.*
I can tell she is starting to fall for Johnny's act.

Obviously, no one has ever treated Cindy tenderly in her life, and
recognizing that makes me incredibly sad. No one has ever treated her

with kindness, or expressing concern with small things like insisting on sunscreen. Clearly, she has lived a hard life and is starving for emotional affection, which makes her catnip for Johnny.

He is enjoying every moment of this vicious game, but the best is yet to come.

Now Johnny starts to go into doctor mode and admonishes poor Cindy for smoking.

"I know you're an adult, and it is really none of my business," Johnny says with paternal concern, "but the only person you are hurting is yourself by smoking. The long-term effects it will have on your lungs are irreversible, and it would be a shame to see you get your life together, only to have cancer then."

"I know," Cindy says, and I can tell she is touched by his concern. "I have been planning on quitting for a while now. It is just a hard habit to break."

"With everything you have told me about your life, I know you are strong enough to do it," he says encouragingly, "you just have to take that first step and stop."

Cindy looks at him for a moment and smiles.

"Your right Johnny, I am going to stop smoking right now." She says with confidence. "Thanks for caring enough to say something to me."

"Good for you!" he says as he smiles broadly, "I am proud of you for having the courage to better yourself."

Cindy's smile lights up the whole room with that comment and even I start to buy Johnny's act a little. After decades of practice, Johnny has become really good at emotional manipulation. He is very skilled at playing the part of "the good guy" without actually doing anything good.

Truth be told, I hadn't figured out most this game out until I thought about it years later. At the time, when you are caught up in something like this and your still struggling to be a decent human being, your goal is to survive it – *and then try and forget about it.* You avoid thinking critically about anything because the more you do, the more you hate yourself for being a part of it.

Now you may be thinking that this doesn't seem so bad. Everyone (but me) is having a good time, right? But the honeymoon is about to be over, and now we are getting to the marriage part of the trip.

And I get no thrill watching decent people suffer.

What I call the "marriage" part of the experience is just what it sounds like, at least marriage to Johnny. The fun is over, and the scales fall away. The mind games start. Once Johnny senses that he has the girl – the moment she gives herself to him – he gets bored and starts to reject her. He is no longer as attentive, demonstrative, and complimentary. He pretends to be bored and acts as if she has done something wrong. He makes sure she feels like it's *her* fault that he is no longer interested.

The poor girl's reaction is always the same. She can't see the game, thanks to years of pain and abuse, all feeding her insecurity. Desperate to win him back, she redoubles her efforts. Each girl has a slightly different way of doing this, but the intention is always the same. She'll do whatever he wants to make him "happy" again, to make him "love" her again.

That night, after a couple of hours with Johnny, Cindy doesn't talk much. She looks totally defeated as she enters my room. I feel guilty because all I am thinking is, *please don't share, please don't share, OH PLEASE DON'T SHARE!*

To my relief, she asks to go to bed early, and I feel a little guilty as I turn out the light.

A short while later, my relief and guilt turn to horror as Cindy experiences an epic nightmare that wakes me up instantly. I can only assume it was caused by whatever happened in Johnny's room. She keeps saying, "No!" and "Stop!" over and over in her sleep. She kicks and punches in her sleep. I turn on the light. She calms down but doesn't wake up.

A single tear rolls down her cheek. I see it, and a rage comes over me that I try to contain. *Who the hell does this guy think he is?* I ask myself furiously.

I know the answer. I know who he is, and I know why I let him put me in this position. *Because I love my grandmother,* I tell myself. While that's the truth, it's not the entire truth. What I am unwilling to see is that I too am being exploited and manipulated. It's not just my best intentions that are being used against me, but my need to be loved.

It took years of counseling to figure that out.

I had no idea back in Vegas. I didn't yet understand the carefully crafted deception Johnny practiced.

After another day trying to make Johnny happy, Cindy starts to look tired, frustrated and depressed. I know she is beating herself up for failing to please him. We are coming to the end of the marriage. Everyone is trying to put on a happy face to mask the disappointment in how the marriage turned out. I think of it as the last Christmas dinner we will spend together before the divorce. Everyone is desperately hoping it will somehow work itself out, even as the parents are planning to call their lawyers after dinner.

That afternoon things go from bad to worse when we bump into a friend of my sister in the hotel gift shop!

How do we explain this? Quickly runs through my mind as Johnny takes off in one direction and Cindy knows enough to keep her distance. I tell my sister's friend I am in Vegas visiting a client by myself and she seems to buy it. After a couple of minute of small talk with the girl, I head back up to my hotel room. In the elevator, I even congratulate myself for helping Johnny dodge a bullet.

My momentary happiness doesn't last long.

Johnny storms into the room a moment later and questions me with a manic energy in his voice. "Who was that girl? Did she see us?" he demands to know. I try to calm him down, but he is spinning out. Whatever he is on is wearing off or making it worse. In a last ditch effort, I tell him I texted my sister and let her know I bumped into her friend to establish an alibi ahead of time. Before I finish my sentence, he screams, "Are you trying to set me up? Did I make a mistake in trusting you?"

After Cindy's heartbreaking nightmares, his irrational mood swings and finding out more about his sexual habits than I want to know, I snap.

"Are you kidding me?" I yell. "I have never, ever played you! And considering the amount of shit I have had to endure to protect your ass, you are lucky I don't throw you through that plate glass window!" My outburst has an effect on him. He backs down and tries another approach;

he plays the "poor me" card, the very same one that sucked me into this mess in the beginning.

It's the same old song, and I buy it every time.

The "poor me" routine goes like this. He can't trust anyone. No one loves or understands him. I should remember how much he trusts me by sharing this secret with me. He even exploits my protective impulses, reminding me how it would kill my grandmother and half sisters if his secret ever got out. I quickly agree with him and tell him that is why I am watching his back.

The sad fact is, even though I know better, I desperately want to believe him. I want to be worthy of his trust, and I don't want to be the person being used. After a brief pep talk from Johnny, we resume our schedule of expensive meals, shows and prepare to wrap up the trip.

After three nights of not sleeping, thanks to Cindy's nightmares and my increasingly guilty conscience, I am counting the hours until this one is over. I am whistling while I pack in the morning and fantasizing about the triple Bloody Mary I am going to have on the plane.

Life is good. I think as I finish the last of my packing. *I made it out of another trip unscathed with no major incidents.*

Then Cindy storms into the room in a rage. And I mean *pissed*!

"Johnny isn't going to pay me!" she screams.

All the oxygen in the rooms is sucked out in an instant. Whatever happiness I felt instantly evaporates.

"ARE YOU KIDDING ME?!"

"No," Cindy says tearfully. "He keeps saying over and over again, 'I just wanted a *girlfriend*.'"

Johnny knocks on my door and asks if he can speak with me for a moment. I ask Cindy to give us a minute.

She sees that I am trying to fix this and may be even more upset than she is, so she waits in the bathroom.

Alone with Johnny, I lower my voice. "Are you out of your mind? I told you I didn't want to be involved with this! What are you doing?"

Johnny acts as if I have betrayed him by siding with Cindy. "She wants a thousand dollars a day, and there is no way she is worth that," he says. "I told her she wasn't getting anything from me."

There are times in life you just want to hit someone and not stop. Luckily my lifetimes worth of experience in dealing with difficult situations starts to kick in, and I go into negotiation mode.

"Look, I told you I didn't want to be involved with this. It isn't fair for you to suck me into it. Just live up to whatever arrangement you made with her!"

Johnny becomes indignant. "We never discussed money! And besides, once a woman crosses state lines, paying a certain amount violates something called The Mann Act. That's a federal crime! I can't pay her."

I am almost speechless, but manage to ask, "Why the hell would you ask someone to fly from Montreal to VEGAS if you didn't take care of it ahead of time?"

Johnny looks at me as a smile crosses his face and he answers my question in a low voice, "I just wanted a girlfriend," he then raises his voice so Cindy can hear in the bathroom, "besides, Soon should have known better than to send me a smoker."

I can hear things starting to break in the bathroom. It is a clear response to what Johnny just said, and my blood pressure is going from bad to worse.

First, he tortures her emotionally and now this?

I am desperate. I don't have the money to cover his debt, and he knows it. He is happy now as I try to bargain. "Listen, just give me the money and I will lend it to her. I will get her to sign an agreement stating it's a loan with interest and tell her don't worry about it! I can sell that."

"No," Johnny says, his anger rising, "she gets nothing. That will teach Soon a lesson for sending me a smoker."

"What the hell is wrong with you?" I ask desperately as I am starting to lose it. "She told me her rent is due the end of this month! This is the money she needs to pay it!"

I can tell from his expression he is enjoying the fact that she is miserable, hurt and angry. He's getting off on her suffering. I have never wanted to hit someone so badly in my life. I hear something shatter in the bathroom. I quickly change tactics, as I know remorse and pity are not in his emotional vocabulary.

"Are you trying to screw me over?" I ask. "The room is in my name!"

"I guess you shouldn't have trusted me," he says as he walks toward the door and turns back to me. "Do whatever you want but she better not bother me again. I am going to my room, and I want to be left alone." He slams the door shut and leaves me standing in the middle of the room completely speechless.

For once, I don't have an answer or solution. Cindy emerges from the bathroom. Before I can start my apology, she says she heard the whole thing. Apparently in my rage at Johnny, my voice went from a whisper to a scream. This poor woman, who now can't afford to pay her rent, has more pity for me than herself.

"Thanks for trying," she says gratefully as she continues to try and calm me down, "I know this isn't your fault. Hell, if I just wanted to sleep with some guy for free, I would have chosen you over some old man."

"Thank you," I mumble in a feeble attempt to acknowledge her compliment, and then I confess that I don't know what else to do. I ask her if she wants to take the cab with me to the airport. She accepts.

When we get into the cab, I keep repeating how sorry I am that this happened, how embarrassed that I even know Johnny, as his actions are despicable. As we talk, I get the feeling she knows a lot more about my relationship with him than I thought. She tries to make me feel better and tells me confidentially that the Soon will make it right when she gets back to Montreal.

As we wait in the airport security line, she even refuses my offer to give her what I have in my wallet.

From the start, I knew Cindy was a good human being trying to make the best out of a bad situation...just as I was. This last gesture shines a light on who she really is, which puts an even greater spotlight on Johnny's character. We part after we get through security, and I can't get to the airport bar fast enough.

I have ten minutes before my plane takes off, but I order a triple shot,

Bloody Mary. The bartender doesn't even raise an eyebrow as I down half the drink as soon as I get it. I tell him to make me another one, as my flight takes off in five minutes and he goes to work.

My burner phone rings and I know who it is before I answer. Johnny. I give him a quick rundown of what happened. Once again, I have cleaned up Johnny's mess, and he has gotten exactly what he wanted with no cost or consequence to himself.

As I hang up the phone and the second Bloody Mary hits my lips, I think about what my grandmother would think of Johnny if she knew the truth. Johnny wasn't lying when he told me that her finding out would kill her and my sisters. It was the main reasons I put myself through the "Johnny Russell Experience" each time, to make sure they never found out.

Still this latest fiasco was a new low, even for Johnny and I start worrying about what might happen on the next trip. Of course, anyone reading this might think of Johnny as a sociopath, a sleazebag, or human cancer. But I can't...

At least not at that moment, because he is my father and I want to protect my family from the truth.

CHAPTER TWO

MONTREAL

I would like to say that the Vegas trip was the worst of it or that it was just some big mistake.

Unfortunately, it was just the beginning of a long and very painful journey to discover who my father really is.

My life didn't start out this way.

When I was young, I saw a very different side of him. All my life, I was raised to believe my father was a selfless doctor, working hard to heal others. He brought life into this world delivering babies day and night. I spent half of my childhood visiting him, sleeping in doctors lounges while he was in the operating room. When he told me to get the phone number of a cute nurse, I could do it in seconds.

As I look back now, I'm not sure if he genuinely enjoyed my company or if I was, even at the age of seven, just a prop for him. But I considered him tireless in his very noble profession, and he was a hero in my eyes.

And what kid doesn't want a hero for a dad? It took too many years for me to shake this image.

But somehow things changed. Did his core character change? Or did I just get to know him better when I became an adult? *I'm still not sure.* But I do know that at some point, the admirable and respected father I knew took too many wrong turns and became the person I call "Johnny Russell" today.

Maybe he changed because he stopped getting everything he wanted.

All of my life, my father told me that there was nothing more important than keeping the "Davis" family line going. I am the last male Davis in our line. The product of an unsuccessful first marriage that did not live up to his expectations, he tried to establish a new line with his current wife, Maria. They had two daughters. Whenever he was upset with Maria, he would remind her that nothing was more important than keeping the "Davis" line going and he had only *me* to do it with now.

My half-sisters, Lisa and Madison, grew up in the shadow of this bastard son, me, in their lives, causing tension between their parents. Maria deeply resented the fact that my father had another wife once and a child with her. She made sure I suffered for this.

Things went from bad to worse during the child custody case. I chose to live with my mother and her new husband instead of with them. I don't know why I made this choice, but I was pressured by both parents, and I guess I just felt safer staying with my mother. On the day the judge awarded custody to my mother, my father's father (whom I loved dearly) died of cirrhosis of the liver. My father told his wife, "I have never felt more alone and unhappy in my entire life."

That single statement elicited an emotional response from Maria that would make him use it for decades to come. She called me that night.

"I just wanted you to know you killed your grandfather with your selfishness!" she snarled at me. "If you had visited him for Christmas, he would still be alive!" She slammed the phone down, leaving me to process what had happened. My wanting to live with my mother was selfishness! And I killed my grandfather!

I was eight years old.

Obviously, I now have the perspective of an adult. I don't blame myself for my grandfather's death, although as the obedient kid, I did then. Being blamed for it had a residual effect on me for years. I decided I'd never be selfish again. I'd be stronger. I was determined to put my family's happiness and safety first, always. If I did this, I figured, I would never be called selfish again. I could help keep peace in the home, and they would value and love me.

It didn't quite work out that way.

So I was raised primarily by my mother and stepfather in Los Angeles, but every summer vacation and holiday, I returned to my father and his wife, Maria, who reminded me every single time what a mistake my father had made in marrying my mother.

Even at that young age, I realized the only reason I was being kept around was to continue the "Davis" family line and because for some unfathomable reason, my grandmother loved me. She watched how they treated me; they didn't dare go too far or be indiscreet with their abuse.

Fast forward several decades. After 30 years of being treated like the bastard stepson, and Maria's personal emotional piñata, I had finally walked out of their lives two years before. I still hoped to have a decent relationship with my father and sisters, but as a man, I just couldn't take it anymore. Unfortunately, my grandmother fell into a great sadness when I stopped visiting, and her health began to deteriorate.

During this time my father lobbied me incessantly to take a bonding trip with him as a way to boost her health and spirits. I had agreed to take the trip as a way to help my grandmother and hopefully build a better relationship with my father. Once I agreed to the trip, he asked me to do him a favor.

He told me he wanted to go to Afghanistan to teach midwives how to deliver children in the outback. He said the family was worried about his safety, and refused to let him go. He needed me to be his alibi, to help him do some good, while sparing his loved one's concern. So, in support of this noble cause, I agreed to lie.

I unknowingly passed his first test.

Montreal, Canada: February 1st, 2011

After enduring a seven-hour flight, I walk to the exit of the airport baggage claim and the electronic door opens. An Arctic blast hits my body, and my eyes sting from the cold as I step outside.

My first thought is that only my father would do something like this, *Montreal in February?* I assume he got some type of deal on the plane tickets, because every time I turned on the news for the last month, all they talked about was, "The Worst Winter in decades."

I look around and jump into a cab quickly. I give the driver the address to where we are staying. I'm a little worried about the accommodations, as my father hates to spend money on anything having to do with me.

I am not a snob by any stretch of the imagination. The first place I ever rented was an efficiency apartment that I couldn't afford to furnish. The first year I lived there, I slept on a feather bed on the floor, until I could save enough money for a used waterbed. Needless to say, my standards are not high, and as long as it is clean and safe, I'll be thrilled.

"Hey buddy, have you heard anything about the place I am staying at?" I ask the cab driver hoping I can get some information on the place before I get there.

"No Mon, but it's a pretty nice neighborhood," the driver replies in a Jamaican/French accent.

I want to ask more questions, but I don't want to distract him, as we have just pulled onto the freeway. Now we are driving in a complete whiteout, and I can't see anything. I tell him I am not in a rush to get there so that he will slow down. Thirty minutes later, we pull up to a really nice Hotel/Condo.

When I get out of the cab, I start to wonder if he dropped me off at the wrong place. This place is really nice. *Too nice.* While I know he might book something like this for my sisters and his wife, there is *no way* he would do it for just me.

I try to shake this negative thought and be positive.

For a moment, I stand in the cold, and I allow myself to think about it... *maybe I am wrong.* Maybe this is some grand gesture. Maybe my father actually is going out of his way to show me he really does care and isn't just going through the motions to please my grandmother!

A frigid gust snaps me out of this fantasy, and I race to the front door of the Hotel.

Once I step into the lobby, I know I have the wrong place. It is even nicer on the inside, and that's when it hits me. My *father* is probably staying here, and I am booked in some place cheaper down the street. That makes a lot more sense to me, and I kick myself for getting my hopes up, as I walk up to the front desk. I assume my father has left a key and directions to where I am staying with them.

"Hey buddy, I just wanted to check if Doctor Davis left something for me. My name is David Davis. I am his son."

"Yes sir. He asked me to give you this and tell you to meet him upstairs in 1217," the desk clerk replies as he looks for a key.

"Thanks, but I would kind of like to check into where I am staying first," I tell him as I take the key and ask, "was there a note or something telling me where I am staying?"

"I believe you are staying here sir. That is the key for 1217," he says and starts looking at me strangely now, as if I should know this.

"Oh...OK. Thanks," I tell him happily as I pick up my bags and head for the elevators. When I step in the elevator, I let my imagination run wild as I can't help but wonder, *Maybe he is really serious about this whole "bonding" thing?* I feel a lump in my throat and my eyes tear up a little at this thought.

It sounds like I am overreacting, but all of my life I had been treated as an "afterthought" by my father. I knew my grandmother was the only reason he even contested my mother's sole custody when I was a child. His actions had let me know I was an obligation to him, not someone he actually valued. This is the first time in my life my father has done something to indicate he really cared about me.

As pathetic as it sounds, this gesture means the world to me.

"Man up and get a hold of yourself!" I tell myself quietly as I walk down the hallway.

I finally pull myself together as I get to 1217. I decide to knock on the door, instead of using my key. My father opens the door, and we walk into the living room. I am totally blown away by this place. It is two bedrooms with a nice living room and a fully functional kitchen.

"How was the trip to Afghanistan?" I ask him trying to sound casual and mask my happiness. I know he is proud of what he has done, and I want to let him brag a little.

Also, it is *our secret,* and I know he won't have anyone else to share it with.

"Great. Let me show you the gift the birth mothers gave me for teaching them," he says as he walks over to a box on the table. He opens it up and shows me a small silver dagger with some Persian writing on the blade.

"That's so cool," I tell him as I hold the dagger carefully, and then I ask him the question I know he wants to answer, "did you run into any trouble while you were there?"

"Other than the bomb that went off two blocks from the hotel I was staying my first night, it wasn't that bad," he tells me about his adventure with a touch of modesty, "they smuggled me into a school where all of the birth mothers had gathered, and I managed to hold two classes before word spread of an American doctor being in the village. Once that happened they had to get me out of there pretty quickly."

"Why?" I ask.

"Most of the Mullahs have made a decree that villagers should kill any foreign doctors that try to teach the birth mothers. They were afraid for my safety. Of course, I wanted to stay, but they were too worried about what might happen to me," he says proudly.

At that moment, I am pretty proud of my father for what I considered this act of courage. The mortality rate for new mothers in Afghanistan is the highest in the world. There is a real lack of medical expertise available in the outer regions that are controlled by the Taliban.

It is also the first time in my life that I have seen him doing something for someone else without any visible benefit to him; I want to be as supportive as I can be of this new side of him. When he first approached me with the idea, I told him I would go with him to watch his back, but he wouldn't hear of it.

Later that night at dinner, I notice something different about my father. At first, he seemed happy to see me, but now he is acting a little bored and edgy. The next morning, he wakes me up very early and tells me that he wants to talk with me for a moment about something important.

Maybe he is thinking about the money he spent on the place, and it is just too expensive to justify spending it on me? I wonder as I try to figure out what is going on. *Has he found a way to get out of paying for the entire week and is going home early?*

Before our talk, he tells me he wants to call my grandmother and tell her about the good time we were having. In my mind, I assume he is going to drop the hammer of canceling the trip after the call. I am already chastising myself for getting my hopes up about this trip, but when I hear my grandmother's voice, I know coming to Montreal was the right thing to do.

"You both have no idea how much it warms my heart to know you both are finally spending time with each other," she says with tears in her voice. "It just makes me so happy." At that moment, my heart melts a little bit. Her voice is what immediately comes to mind whenever I think of kindness.

After a couple of minutes, I can tell my father is getting bored with the conversation, and he ends the call quickly. I brace myself for what is coming next. I have already decided that if he wants to cancel the trip, I simply ask him to keep it between us. Grandma deserves to be happy, and it's just a *little lie.*

I brace myself for the worst, but I have no clue what is coming.

"I am going to take you to a place where you can do whatever you want, a massage parlor," he tells me in a serious tone. "There's a relationship between men and women that has been going on forever, and it's something I want to share with you..."

As he continues his speech, the volume of his voice drops out, as my defense mechanisms kick into high gear, and rapid-fire questions start filling my mind. *What do I do? How do I react? If I say no thanks, how will he react? Will I get kicked out of the family for good this time?*

I snap back to reality as I hear him ask, "If you have any questions..."

I interrupt him quickly, "Dad, sure! No worries, I get it! Let's go."

It is hard to describe what I am feeling right now. I am not processing everything because I know he is watching me and evaluating how I'm handling this one. The physical reaction feels like getting kicked in the stomach and slapped in the face at the same time. That kind of stunned energy that comes from absorbing a hit you never saw coming.

I can't even process my mental reaction, and I just put everything on hold. I know I have to get through whatever comes next and think about it later. We put on our cold weather gear and head out the door. He tells me to dress warm, as we are going to walk to the place from the hotel.

How does a guy that has never been to a brothel agree to it that quickly?

It's simple. A long, long time ago I started to suspect that if it came down to making a choice, in my father's eyes I was ultimately expendable. Although he said he cared about me, I knew it was only because I was the last male "Davis" in our line and my grandmother loved me. I know I am on shaky ground with him right now, and there are wide ranging consequences for saying, "No thanks."

On the elevator ride downstairs, I think about the conversation we just had with my grandmother. My father said all the right things, assuring her that we were having a good time. She probably imagined us doing father-son stuff, maybe going to a movie or dinner. Instead, he hangs up the phone and takes me *to a brothel.*

I had hoped I could reconnect with my father in some way, establish a good relationship with him, and make my grandmother happy. That was the plan. Now I have no clue what to do. As we walk out the front door into the arctic blizzard, I start to think about the consequences of just saying no thanks.

I desperately don't want to lose my family again, as had happened years earlier after I stood up to his wife, Maria. Almost immediately, I was isolated from the family. Even my sisters, with whom I'd thought I had a pleasant relationship, ignored me. I called them every three weeks for three years, only to have those calls go unreturned.

My greatest concern is my grandmother. I know if I don't "play along," my father will immediately consider me a threat to his relationship with her. While I don't think he will be able to cut me out of her life, he will force her to choose between us and I can't allow that. Even though I know she will choose to keep me in her life, my father and Maria will hold it against her; it is their way. Also, my grandmother's health has totally rebounded since I agreed to take this trip.

Somewhere deep inside of me, the memory of what happened to my grandfather opens up and at that moment I know I can't be responsible for anything bad happening to my grandmother. As irrational as it sounds, I am simply unwilling to risk hurting her by putting what is in my own best interest first.

The final factor in making my decision is the one I can't even admit to myself. The truth is this is the first time my father has ever really reached out to me in my life and shared something of a personal nature. As twisted as it sounds, I don't want to let him down by not understanding what he is trying to share with me.

As a son, I want to be there for him, and I want to be someone he can count on. At the same time, I know this is not normal, and there is something very wrong with my father. I have no clue what a good son does in this type of situation, and I am panicked.

Why is he sharing this with his son? I ask myself as we walk through the blizzard. *Is this actually something that happens a lot with fathers and their sons, but no one talks about it?*

Twenty minutes after getting off the phone with my grandmother, my father and I walk into a building that houses the massage parlor/brothel. As we get off the elevator on the fourth floor, a well-dressed woman gives us a look. I've never been looked at like this before, and I instantly feel dirty; it is like she knows what we are about to do.

I find out later that prostitution, while technically illegal, is generally accepted in Montreal. Operating under the guise of massage parlors, brothels often share office building space with legitimate businesses. Some of the business owners are less than thrilled about "Johns" walking in and out of their buildings. This look is a subtle reminder of that fact.

It is my first experience of what it feels like to be a "John," and *I already want to kill myself.*

This, of course, brings up my father's alter ego "Johnny Russell." It is the name he uses to disguise himself in whorehouses and massage parlors.

Johnny (get it? A "John") combined with "Russell," which, he explained to me during our quick, cold walk to the brothel, is our *real* last name.

At the time, I had no idea that my grandfather's real surname was Russell. Apparently, he couldn't claim the name because he was born out of wedlock and his father was already married. When Mike Russell, my father's grandfather, passed away, he left his son two ranches– but not his last name.

Now I am beginning to realize why having our "Davis" family line go on is really so important to my father. It legitimizes my grandfather in my father's eyes.

I am processing this latest information as we walk toward the door of the massage parlor when "Johnny" turns to me and lets me know he has already talked to the girls about me. He has told them that I'm his brother.

HIS BROTHER! Okay, I get that he doesn't want to appear old enough to have a son my age but....

Doesn't he know how sick and twisted this is? I ask myself as my mind is racing as I struggle to find reasons my father would share this with me. *Maybe he just testing my character or loyalty?*

My father doesn't seem to notice that I am fighting a wave of dread. He has this excited look on his face now, a look that I can only assume is anticipation.

I'm getting a sick feeling that nothing I hoped would happen during this bonding trip will actually come to pass. Worse, I can't even properly process what is going on.

This guy is a doctor doing good works in Afghanistan! I think to myself. *A church going, honorable member of society! This is how he spends his free time?*

"You know Maria found this place for me," he says casually as he opens the door to the brothel.

Maria hooks him up with whorehouses? I think as I swallow my surprise and start to think through this latest bombshell.

As we walk inside, it is starting to make a little sense to me now. With me isolated from the family, I am the perfect beard for my father's double life. I have been raised my entire life with the core value that a man does whatever he can to protect his family. *Who could my father and Maria trust more than his own son?*

Inside the Massage Parlor is a depressing mix of old Asian prints on the wall and used office furniture. There are a bunch of shoes sitting next to the front door. The whole place is sad and rundown. My father starts to run me through the drill.

"Take off your shoes and put on the sandals," he tells me, and I look at the pile of dirty sandals by the door. As I start to put them on, I am already thinking about the showers I am going to take after I get out of there.

Soon, a heavy-set Asian woman, comes out of a back office to greet us.

"You must be Johnny's brother David!" she says warmly. "He has told me so much about you. It's nice to meet you!"

Soon smiles and seems to be going out of her way to make me feel comfortable. It is as if she knows it's my first time and that makes me even more uncomfortable. At that moment, I want the floor to open up and swallow me, but I manage to mumble, "Hello."

"I have someone very special for you!" she tells me, as she walks back toward what I assume is a waiting area for the women and calls out, "Janet, get ready. I have someone I want you to meet."

How the hell do I get out of this? I wonder desperately. *Think, damn it!*

Before I can come up with anything, a young 30-year-old Hispanic woman walks into the room, and I freeze in place. My initial dread turns to relief as she walks up to my father and says, "Johnny, where have you been?" as they embrace. Obviously, she isn't "my" girl and my muscles relax a moment.

At least I hope she isn't my girl! I think to myself nervously, as my body starts to go rigid again and my stomach turns.

I stare at my father once he separates himself from her. He looks like he is enjoying every minute of this Father/Son bonding experience and smiles at me. I manage a weak smile back, while every fiber of my being is screaming, "*GET OUT OF HERE NOW!!! RUN!!*"

The door to the room that this girl walked out of remains open and I can hear the movie *Twilight* playing.

Is that how these women keep it together working here, I start to wonder? *By believing that their "Edward" is out there somewhere?*

I snap out of this thought when a blond woman in her 30s walks out of the waiting room and Soon introduces me to her.

"This is Janet. She is from California, like you!" Soon says and I feel like I am having an out of body experience as I barely manage a "Hello."

My father hangs out with his "girl" to see if we get along. I feel like everyone is watching me, and I don't know what to do.

"Are you ready for your massage?" Janet asks me, and I just nod weakly as we all go to rooms in the back. "Johnny" walks into his room with his "girlfriend" and I follow Janet into hers.

Janet also seems to sense this is a first for me and is very nice about it. She asks me to take off my clothes and lie down on a bed that has no box spring under it, just a removable cover like in a doctor's office with a sheet folded up in the middle of the mattress.

In the room next to me, I can hear "Johnny" having a good time with his "girlfriend." I try to block out the sounds coming from next door, but I can't. This is just wrong on every level, and I know it.

Just get through it and you can figure it out later, I think to myself, as I try to ignore what is happening next door.

I would like to say I figured out a way out of it at the last moment, but I didn't. While I didn't pay for anything (my father had very specifically told me not to), I did have sex with Janet. I was sure he would check. I got out of there as quickly as possible and jogged back to the condo.

After my third shower, I am about to wash my clothes for a second time, when I get a call from my father. He is still at the brothel and wastes no time with his questions.

"You had sex with her! What were you thinking?"

"That's what you brought me there for!" I reply defensively.

"I took you there to meet her and see how you feel about her," he says quickly as his voice rises. "I hadn't even tested her yet!"

Of course, this immediately freaks me out, and I practically shout. "Test her for *what*?"

"AIDS!" he practically screams.

My heart is now racing. Of course I used a condom, but the way he is acting isn't helping my already active imagination. Before I can think of a reply, he tells me, "Don't worry about it. I have already tested her, but you have to let me test them first. I'm looking out for you!"

Yes, my father, who has gotten me involved in the single most screwed up thing I have ever done in my life, just said that to me.

He's looking out for me. I think to myself. *This is the father I have been dreaming about all of my life, the one who tests hookers for AIDS to "protect" his son.*

Father of the year!

Years later, when I am being rushed into trauma surgery, my life will flash before my eyes. Trusting my father and participating in his little bonding experience would be the thing I regret the most, the one thing I wish I could un-live.

That night at dinner, after spending the entire day at the brothel, my father is over the moon. He can't stop talking about the adventures we are going to have and how happy he is to share all this with me.

This is the first time he seems happy to be with me. I keep thinking. *For my entire life, he has never fully accepted me, never taken the time to know me. But now that I have done this, I am one of the guys, and suddenly worth having around!*

As much as I love my grandmother and want a relationship with my father, I don't think I can handle this. I feel like the black sludge that collects at the bottom of a New York garbage can after twenty years of being used, but never cleaned. I start thinking about getting on a plane, getting out of there and not looking back.

I think my father can sense how disturbed I am because he tells me the main reason he has shared this with me. He wants to make sure he is covered in case something happens to him at the brothel. What if he strokes out? Has a heart attack? It's my duty as a son, grandson, and brother to make sure my sisters and his mother never find out the truth.

As we walk back to the condo from our dinner, I think about what my father just told me. I know it would kill my grandmother if she found out. This is a woman who practically lived at our church.

I also think about my father. He has trusted me with this huge secret, and I know he isn't going to stop.

Maybe he is reaching out to me in some way, and I just don't see it! I think to myself as I lie in bed that night. *How am I going to keep my grandmother happy, "bond" with my father and still stay out of the brothels?*

I had to come up with some kind of plan.

Unfortunately, I didn't come up with a reason to stay out of the brothel soon enough, and I find myself walking with him to it the next night. Unknowingly, I start to lay some groundwork to avoid the place by complaining about the cleanliness of the place.

"Maria and I have been complaining about it for years," he agrees as we walk toward the massage parlor/brothel and then he tells me, "we have even brought them our old linens, but it doesn't seem to do any good."

Suddenly, I get an idea as we pass several strip clubs. "What about going to a strip club instead?" I ask my father hopefully.

"Strip clubs are a huge waste of money," my father snaps back quickly, and I try to mask my disappointment as we walk into the building that houses the brothel.

An hour later as I start to head out of the brothel, I look at the mirror before I leave. At that moment, I know I am not going to be able to handle coming back here again. While I am the opposite of delicate, and I love the company of women, this is just wrong. I know I have to figure out a way to sidestep this part of the bonding experience without offending him, or I am going to lose it.

As I jog past another strip club on the way home, I am struck with an idea that I hit my father with the next night.

"I am not going with you tonight. If anyone needs me, they have my phone number. I'm going to hit a strip club instead," I tell my father as soon as he gets back from his afternoon trip to the brothel. "It is just a different vibe and a little more hygienic."

"That's ok I guess, but remember you are still on call in case something happens," he says sharply as he gets ready to spend the rest of his night at the brothel.

He really is obsessed with that place, I think to myself, as I head out the door to try to find a strip club to establish an alibi.

My plan was simple: get as far away from what my father was doing as soon as possible and figure out what just happened. I am fully aware that a strip club wasn't the perfect answer, but it was the only answer I could give him, that would make him comfortable enough to leave me alone.

Also, I *really* needed a drink ... or twelve! I had been sober for a while, but I needed to escape what I was feeling as quickly as possible. Alcohol was the fastest, most reliable way for me to numb out and I know it.

I have had a problem with drinking most of my life, but up to this point, I haven't dealt with it properly. When I confessed my problem to the family years before, they exploited it as best they could, revealing my secret to any and all and weakening my credibility with my grandmother. Looking back on it, I suspect my father had little interest in seeing me get well as it strengthened his position with my grandmother and her money.

On the street that night, I am one of the few people walking as the blizzard continues to blow through Montreal. This is not my first time at a strip club, and the people seem nice enough. As I have said before, I am not a saint or delicate, but having my father share this with me is just too much to handle.

I need a drink in the worst way.

A hostess shows me to a table, as the techno/dance music blares on the sound system and the DJ introduces the next dancer. I order a double Cape Cod and down it as soon as it hits the table. I immediately order another one and start thinking about the problem I face before I slip into a welcome oblivion...

CHAPTER THREE

ALISON MEETS DAVID RUSSELL

A STRIP CLUB!!!

How did I get here? I think to myself as the music blares in the background; my mind replays what just happened. *I came to Montreal to build a better relationship with my father and boost my grandmother's health and spirits! Now I am hiding out in a STRIP CLUB because it is the only thing I could come up with to keep me out of my father's FAVORITE BROTHEL!!!*

How did things go so wrong, so quickly and what the hell is wrong with my father? I ask myself for the hundredth time. *I am not married, but I can't believe this is something that fathers normally do with their single sons.*

Maybe it's my job? I think to myself.

I work in the entertainment industry, but it isn't exactly like what people see on *Entourage*, and he knows it. I run my own company as a talent manager where I deal with artistic personalities often navigating impossible situations, but I spend most of my time finding them work, negotiating their contracts and generally guiding their careers.

Maybe, I think, as I struggle to find some insight into my father's thinking, *the hedonistic, self-indulgent image of Hollywood made my father think it was perfectly acceptable to share this sleazy dark side with me.*

But what the hell do I do now? I wonder as I start drinking my third double Cape Cod.

At that moment, I wish with all my might that my father and I were out bonding the normal way, maybe fishing or hunting together. The truth is, I have no clue how I am even going to handle this...

I haven't even heard of something like this! My mind races, as I search for some type of solution.

I know I can't turn my back on him. He is my father, and although we have never had a close relationship, he obviously needs my help. He came to me with this for some reason, and I want to be there for him, but I also realize the risk I am taking. There are only so many showers a man can take and times he can wash his clothes; some stains you can't wash out.

Pull yourself together and stop feeling sorry for yourself! I think to myself angrily. *You deal with impossible situations all of the time. Man up and deal with it!*

This thought knocks me into manager mode, and I start to analyze what I have seen so far. Immediately, a number of worse case scenarios flash through my mind and his actions have made them all very real concerns.

Having my 79-year-old father being found dead of a heart attack in a brothel is at the top of the list. When we talked about what to do if this happens, he showed me the underground elevator entrance where we were staying, the day after my first visit to the brothel.

"There are no cameras at the entrance, and you can carry me to the elevator and get me to the room with no one seeing," my father told me, as we retraced the route back to the brothel from the entrance.

While I know there is something very wrong with my father, we don't have the kind relationship where I feel I can ask him direct questions. We rarely speak and on the odd occasions we do, it is always about my grandmother or work. The only real conversations I have ever had with him was when I was a kid. I search my mind for some insight into what might have set him on this path.

I know he has some pretty strange views about marriage.

He told me "the truth about women" when I was ten years old. We were with his friends at a block party BBQ. The guests there were very well-educated, high status, upper-class members of Texas society. We lived two doors down from the former first lady, Lady Bird Johnson, who had both a helicopter pad at her house and her own secret service detail.

It was that type of neighborhood.

There I was, a kid surrounded by the most successful judges, doctors, lawyers and bankers in Texas, when my father told me, "What you have to understand, son, is that no woman will ever be honest with you. They'll say and do whatever it takes to get you to marry them. Only then will you see the real person come out, and by then it is too late! You're married!"

It had sounded like a death sentence.

All of the other men nodded in grim agreement. I got the first confirmation of the heavy price my father paid for trying to continue the "Davis" family line.

"You can never trust them," he said, "because they're only waiting for you to say something they can use against you later."

That supported the narrative my father had established very early in my childhood about being trapped by his wife, and by women in general. Since I was ten years old, I guess he felt I would understand this key intelligence about women: never trust them or I would be trapped.

Just like him.

Throughout my youth, I thought about how selfless my father was in sacrificing his happiness to build a family. He was obviously trapped in an unhappy marriage, but he couldn't leave his wife without destroying my sisters. Maria knew how much he valued his daughters and that he would never leave her.

My father was always the victim in the stories he told me as a kid, and I had been given no reason to doubt him.

Like Maria's accusation of my killing my grandfather, his advice stayed with me for decades. It not only weakened my ability to trust women in relationships but also made me excuse my father's shortfalls as a man.

At that moment in the strip club, I actually felt sorry for my father. I figured he was just trying to find what little scraps of affection he could in the most sordid and depressing places on the planet because he had no other options.

Also, I didn't know if this was some type of weird bonding ritual he had done with my grandfather or where he picked this up. I had a hard time believing my grandfather would do something like this, but if someone had told me three days ago my dad would be taking me to a brothel, I would have said, "You're out of your mind!"

Maybe, I thought, *this type of thing happens in a lot of long-term relationships. The marriage becomes one of convenience.*

Maria obviously approved this arrangement by enabling and containing this behavior. I could see her being more concerned with where he did things than what he was doing. To a woman like Maria, appearances are everything. If it looks good, it must *be* good.

So *that's* why we were in Montreal in February.

And that's why my father and Maria took all those exotic trips (to Thailand, Vietnam, etc.). The further away "Johnny" did his thing, the less likely he was ever to get caught or cause a scandal. My mind was spinning while I tried to fill in the gaps of what I didn't know, with what I had been shown and told so far.

The way Maria acted when this trip was being set up (sending confirmation of the travel plans from a new email address, etc.) and his confirming she picked out the whorehouses made me believe she knew, but she never said anything directly to me. It was the perfect setup; the situation was handled, and Maria no longer had to get her hands dirty. She had passed the baton to me without saying a word.

The more I drank, the more impossible the whole thing was becoming, and it was starting to hurt my head to think about it. I have been entrusted with this huge secret, and I know I have to protect him and my family. Now that the alcohol has calmed me down, I start making a plan on *how* I am going to manage this situation.

I know I can't go back to the brothel, and that means coming up with an excuse that will satisfy my father. The excuse has to demonstrate I am not condemning his actions by not participating, and I know the strip club is a temporary fix. The DJ starts introducing the next dancer as I rack my brain for an answer.

"I want everyone to put their hands together and give a special welcome to Alison on our center stage, one of the newest dancers at The Babylon Club. Let's hear it for Alison..." the DJ says in a baritone voice as the music starts to fade in.

I barely pay attention to Alison until she starts to dance.

Alison starts a routine that is a combination of ballet mixed with burlesque. She gives off a very different vibe from the other dancers while she is dancing. She is "authentic" for lack of a better word, dancing, not selling. She seems to be dancing for herself, for the joy of it, just a human being trying to express herself.

At that moment, I have an idea that might just give me the excuse I need to stay out of the brothel.

I started talking with Alison later that night; it was clear that she was a real person, not just playing the part. Most strippers create, along with a fake name, a completely fake personality to go along with it. This creates a barrier between the customer and the dancer, protecting who she "really" is and her private life.

I am not an expert on strippers by any means, but I met quite a few of them working my way through college as a bouncer, bartender, and waiter in Texas. I knew most of them were good people just trying to make ends meet. They looked at dancing as a very temporary thing. By the end of my time in time in Texas, I not only got a degree in business management from Texas State but a real education on people from all walks of life as well.

It was this education that made me not judge Alison, based on what she did for a living.

The more I talked to her, the more taken I was by her extraordinary honesty, and it made me relax a little bit in that environment. Physically, she was a beautiful woman, but it was "who" she was inside that really opened my eyes. Talking to her reminded me that sometimes good people get caught up in bad situations – and of course, that really resonated with me at the time.

In her, I saw a kindred spirit, not an object of sexual satisfaction.

I paid for lap dances as a way to keep her talking to me, but that was all I paid for. I knew I had to play the part, and I was desperate to stay out of the brothel at this point. I made a decision to keep things strictly platonic. It may be a thin line, but it was very important that I not cross it. In addition to really liking Alison, I hoped she could help me preserve what was left of my self-respect and soul.

My plan was simple. If I could get Alison to pretend to be my "girl-friend," it would give me the excuse I needed to stay out of the brothel.

The irony of my situation was the beard now needed a beard.

As a manager, I have made my living coming up with solutions to impossible problems. I always handled the behind the scenes drama and eccentric personalities with a results-oriented approach. I prided myself on my ability to come up with solutions that work and not letting emotions override what was best for all involved.

The biggest problem I faced in dealing with this situation is the fact that this was my father I was dealing with and not a client.

As my mind wandered over all of the possibilities, I realized that I need a lot more information about "why" my father is doing this, but my immediate problem was convincing Alison to hang out with me for the remainder of the trip.

I mentioned to Alison that I was in town for three more days and asked if she was working tomorrow. She gave me her cell number, and I gave her the number of my burner phone. We started texting each other that night and made plans to meet back at the strip club the following night.

Most strippers will never meet you anywhere except the strip club, but I was desperate. I hoped I could convince Alison that I was a good guy and that she would be safe with me. She was the perfect excuse to keep me out of the brothel. I believed keeping up this pretense would buy me the time to figure out what was going on with my father.

Even with a rough idea of how to handle this situation, I still felt like I was treading water with 50-pound weights attached to my legs. The same thought kept on looping over and over in my head, *Gut it out, get to dry land and figure out what to do from there.*

The next night, Alison decided to hang out with me after work, and I introduced her to "Johnny." After five minutes of conversation, his curiosity was now satisfied with my "girlfriend," he promptly left us to return to the brothel. It and whoever he was "dating" became his sole focus on this trip. He could hardly hide his impatience with anything that kept him apart from them.

His latest "girlfriend" was a really nice woman named Patricia. She looked a lot like a 20-year-old version of his current wife Maria, and I was shocked by the physical similarity. I assumed most people who cheat on their wives would look for the exact opposite of their wives, but I later found this is pretty common.

As for Patricia herself, she was extra nice to me. She probably thought that if she could win me over, she would be one step closer to landing "Johnny" in a more serious relationship. For my part, I tried to be as nice a possible given the situation, but our interactions gave the word "awkward" a whole new meaning.

While getting ready for a fourth night out on the town, my father finally opened up to me a little bit.

"You know Patricia gives me back half my money every time I visit her," my father tells me.

"Half?" I ask not sure if I heard him correctly.

"The house keeps the other half. She explained how the whole setup works to me the other night," he responds with a pride in his voice that kills me a little.

"Why don't you just meet her at the condo?" I ask absently, my mind still reeling at the conversation we are having.

"They aren't allowed to come back to the condo and Soon doesn't like them leaving the brothel," he says with a strange look on his face now.

"I guess that makes sense," I say, relieved that they won't be coming to the condo and mentally kicking myself for asking the question. However, I get a sick feeling in my stomach as I look over at my father and recognize the excited look on his face. It's the same one he had when we were in the brothel that first time.

Four days into the trip and our quality time had already been reduced to a quick breakfast. Then he raced to the brothel. We'd meet for lunch and then he ran back to the brothel. A quick dinner and he would end his night at the brothel.

As for me, I spent my time in between breakfast, lunch and dinner reading at the condo. At night, I hit the strip club. I had to keep up my cover with Alison, and we were quickly becoming friends. I told her outright she was never expected to "do anything." I found myself looking forward to spending time with Alison, either at the strip club or going out to eat.

"You know, your brother is a little strange, right?" Alison asks me in her French-accented English.

"You don't even know the half of it!" I reply quickly, but a little too loud. We were at the strip club, and the music is deafening.

"Is that why you never bring him here?" she asks. At that moment, I wanted to tell her the truth but say, "That and I would rather spend my time with you." Luckily she is up next to dance, and we never finish the conversation.

The next evening at dinner, Alison and I talked, really talked, about her life choices and what she was doing. I hoped I would have a little credibility with her at this point because I have kept everything completely plutonic between us.

"Don't take this the wrong way, but have you ever thought about doing something else for a living?" I ask her. We are in a nice French restaurant with a romantic vibe, and I am on my fourth Cape Cod of the evening. I have become so relaxed around Alison, that I am debating telling her who "Johnny" really is.

I don't know if it is just the insane situation I am in, but I have a really strong desire to connect with someone at this point. Although it goes against my original plan, I have to admit that I am starting to develop feelings for her.

She has the prettiest crooked smile and green eyes with just a hint of mischief in them. She is a very attractive young woman, who tells me she is 27, but her beauty isn't the only thing that attracts me to her. What I liked most about her is her honesty.

"My family also hates what I do for a living," she says as she takes a sip of her wine and continues. "I love my family, so a couple of years ago I got a job in the 'cubical' world, and they were happy. But I hated the 'cubical' world. It drained me, and I never had time to dance."

"Can't you do ballet or something?" I ask.

"I started in ballet, but you can't make a living doing it unless you get into the right company. I just wasn't good enough to get into the right company," she says sadly. "This is just what works for me now."

At this point, I really didn't like the idea of Alison stripping for a living, as ironic as that might sound. The thought of her working a 9 to

5 job makes me happy. Seeing her being objectified at the club is really starting to bother me. She is a person, not an object to be used, and then tossed aside.

I decided to be honest in a world where honesty does not exist.

The night before I left Montreal, I sent Alison a long text telling her exactly how I felt. I felt like the biggest cliché as I wrote, but I meant every word: she didn't have to live this life, I would help her. She needed to keep chasing her dreams and not let the rejection of the big ballet companies dictate how she was going to live her life.

By morning, there was still no reply from Alison. I walked down the street for a cup of coffee, and when I got back to the condo, I see my father has made himself breakfast. Both of our bags are already packed and sitting by the front door.

My father is really happy and lets me know. "I have to say I have had a great time on this trip, and we have to do it again soon. When I get home, I will start looking into the next trip we can take together!"

I just smile and start to think about it as we finish breakfast. We have spent about fifteen percent of the trip eating meals together. The rest of the time he has been at the brothel. Everything I had hoped for on this trip has been ruined and now I just want to go home.

After I finish breakfast, I head to the door, and he mentions taking another trip again, and I say, "That sounds good, Dad! Let me know what you are thinking about when you get home."

As I walk through the lobby, I can't wait to get outside. Even though the bitter cold takes my breath away, when I step outside, I experience a sense of relief that I haven't felt since this trip began. I hail a taxi and start to feel all of the tension melt away on the cab ride to the airport.

At the airport, I send one more text to Alison from the airport bar. I write that I am sorry if the text from last night upset her, but I meant every word of it. I will help her, and I will be there for her if she wants to get out. I am obsessed with doing something *good* on this trip as everything I have done so far seems wrong.

Maybe helping her is my chance to make amends for being involved what my father has done? I think as I order another drink.

An hour later, I still don't have a reply from her.

As they call out my flight for boarding, I slam down my last Bloody Mary and head toward the gate. I look at the phone one more time, but there is still no reply from Alison. I toss my phone into a trash can as I board the plane.

Maybe my father was right about everything after all. I think to myself as the stewardess starts the seatbelt demonstration. *Maybe this was just the way things worked.*

I did a lot of thinking and soul-searching after the first trip with my father.

"WHAT THE HELL IS WRONG WITH HIM AND WHY DID HE INVOLVE ME IN THIS?!" I asked myself over and over and over. *How had I gone from being his son to being the brother/beard/cleaner?*

Overriding all this inner turmoil was my concern for not only my grandmother's health but her happiness. I generally called her once a week to check in on her, and I had started to notice that she was falling into a depression. Until I agreed to take this trip with my father, she sounded like a shadow of her former self.

One of the first female jockeys in the world, Wanda Davis was a ground breaking rider who beat some of the best male jockeys in horse racing. She defeated Johnny Longden (the top male jockey at the time) at a match race in Agua Caliente and was a legend in her time.

She was the opposite of prideful and anytime a person asked her about racing; she would always say, "Oh it was nice and all, but let me tell you about my grandchildren...."

After my grandfather had died, she ran our 900-acre family ranch on her own in Oklahoma. She named every one of the cattle she raised, and I believe I inherited the caretaking part of my personality from her. She woke up at 4 in the morning and worked until 7 pm every day of her life on the ranch.

In the early 1980s, oil was discovered on the ranch, and while my grandmother wasn't concerned with money, I do believe this is where my father's obsession with money started. While she lived modestly, my father liked to spend money and after his residency, he bought an airplane, a mansion in the hills, and a Lotus Turbo Esprit.

I never thought about it at the time, but I am now convinced a lot of my grandmother's money went toward supporting my father's extravagant lifestyle. I don't see how he could have afforded any of these luxury items so soon after graduating medical school.

The closest my grandmother came to spending money was investing it in businesses my father would ask her to support. He has done very well over the years, building medical offices, buying real estate and living the high life.

When my grandmother had finally retired from working the ranch to live closer to my sisters, she rented a small house from my father and Maria.

"Your grandmother pays us far less rent than the market value of the house," Maria would always point out whenever they fixed something that was broken in it as if her accumulated wealth had nothing at all to do with my grandparents' lifetime of labor.

The house Wanda rented was small, but located across from a school where she could watch the children play. The inside was spartan, to say the least: no fancy furniture, a bed that was twenty years old and a couch. My grandmother had more money than anyone in the family but was a Depression-era baby.

She drove the same Buick for 25 years, taking great pride in not being wasteful and saving her money. When I was little, I used to think she bought special towels: the ones she used were threadbare and thin (after so many washings they had lost their texture) but in her mind they were still good.

Every memory from my childhood that involves her reminds me of the fact she is the kindest, most honest, and compassionate human being that I have ever met.

"It embarrasses your father and Maria," she said, as she showed me a t-shirt she had won by cutting of the tags off dog food bags, "but it is a really good shirt, so I wear it when they are not around."

It is memories like this which are making it tougher and tougher to keep dodging my grandmother's questions on our weekly calls.

"When are you going on another trip with your father?" is the first question she asks me each week and I can hear the hope and happiness in her voice as she continues. "He keeps telling me what a good time you two had and how well you are doing now in business. It makes my heart so happy you both are finally spending time together after all of these years!"

In a weird way, those calls solidified my becoming my father's brother/beard/cleaner, David Russell. In my mind, it would have been too selfish to walk away, taking the risk she might find out the truth about "Johnny." At 92 years old, my grandmother's health and happiness were simply more important to me than my own.

Once I agreed to take another trip, I am my father's new best friend. He tells me he can't wait to see me again! We talk every week, and he is genuinely excited to hear from me. I can hear the energy in his voice and I can tell he is really happy to speak to me, and not just going through the motions.

Is that all it took? Spending a weekend as his brother/beard/cleaner was all I needed to do to get him to value me as a son? I ask myself every time I hang up the phone.

Over the weeks, I try not to think too much about *why* he is happy to be speaking with me, or about the trip's silver lining. I continue to rationalize my actions with my grandmother's happiness, the fact I will be watching his back and that I am protecting my family from the truth.

However, being caught between my love for my grandmother and my father's disgusting idea of a good time is taking its toll.

As soon as I returned to Los Angeles, my drinking increased expo-nentially. From the second I got off the plane, I started to really hit the bottle.

For the first time in my life, my drinking started to affect my work. I find it impossible to sleep, and there is no one I can talk to about this. As a man, it's not like you can turn to a pal and ask, "Hey buddy, has your father ever taken you to a brothel and then asked you to be his brother/ beard/cleaner?"

If I don't have a bottle of wine at night, I find myself staring at the ceiling until morning obsessing over what I have done, wondering who my father really is.

I share DNA with this guy – what does that say about who I am? I keep wondering late at night before the wine finally kicks in.

When I tell my father I'm having problems sleeping, he tells me to ask my doctor to prescribe me Trazodone, an older sleep medication with less addictive qualities. The sleep medication coupled with a couple of glasses of wine seems to do the trick; it lessens the nightmares I suffered since the first trip.

I didn't realize how bad the nightmares were until my friend Alex crashed on my couch one night while his place was being redone. I told him I occasionally talk in my sleep, and snore, but I would keep the door closed to my room.

The next morning I catch Alex just staring at me and ask, "Something I can help you with?"

"You really don't remember?" he asks.

"Remember what?"

Alex looks at me for a second longer, like he is making up his mind whether to tell me or not.

"You scared the shit out of me last night," he finally says, shaking his head as he continues. "I had just fallen asleep when you started screaming at the top of your lungs. I thought the place was being robbed, and you were fighting the burglar."

"You're kidding, right?" I ask, but his face tells me he is dead serious.

"No way man, it took me a moment to realize you were having a nightmare," Alex says, and I can tell it really freaked him out as he continues. "I walked to your bedroom and opened the door. I couldn't make out what you were saying, but it sounded like you were arguing with someone. You literally screamed at the top of your lungs for thirty minutes."

"Sorry you had to go through that. I'll take an extra sleeping pill tonight to make sure I don't have another one," I tell him as I try to end the conversation.

"Take two, buddy. I don't want you to have a heart attack in your sleep," he says as he finishes his coffee.

We eat the rest of breakfast in silence, but I catch him looking at me a couple of more times. It really starts to bother me, because it seems like Alex feels sorry for me. Like he somehow knows what I am going through.

That marked the beginning of my knowing about my "night terrors." I mentioned them to my father and asked him if it was a side effect of the sleeping pills. He told me that I had them since I was a kid, but when I asked my mom, she told me she had no clue what I was talking about!

She suggested I see someone about it, but I told her not to worry. I was the person people went to with their problems, not someone who sought the help or advice from others. I was single, running my own business (which seemed to be my sole focus) and didn't have time for what I perceived as this terrible weakness.

In my mind, a man didn't complain about his problems, he just learned to live with them.

Years later, I would hear a saying in AA that stuck with me, *"The more you resist, the more it persists."* I was resisting looking honestly at what my father was doing and the emotional toll it was taking on me. As a man, I felt it was my duty just to handle it and move on.

The problem with burying your emotions is that it is just a temporary fix: they have to go somewhere. What I didn't address properly in my waking moments came out in the form of "night terrors," and the longer I ignored it, the worse they got. Several months later, I hadn't had a good night's sleep since they started and I was getting desperate.

I needed to talk to someone.

One night at my brother-in-law's bar, I'd had enough alcohol to give me the courage to ask someone if this had ever happened to them. It was a couple of weeks before my next "bonding" trip with my father, and I couldn't stop thinking about it.

I asked my brother in law's friend Matt if he had ever heard about a father taking his son out for a night on the town with hookers. I tried to keep it as vague as possible, and I figured this guy was in the night club business and wouldn't be too shocked.

Man, was I wrong.

"Hell no! What type of screwed up person would do something like that with his son?" Matt instantly replied in a tone that conveyed both his shock and disgust at the thought of something like that. But it was the look he gave me that made me not ask the question for another year and a half; it was the same look Alex gave me.

The last thing I wanted was someone's pity.

After that night, I tried to convince myself that this was something people did but just didn't talk about. Besides, I kept reminding myself, my grandmother was really happy, and her health was better than it had been in years. Also, I was only watching my father's back, not participating. My family's health and happiness were worth taking the hit.

Weren't they?

CHAPTER FOUR

BACK IN MONTREAL

Then Vegas happened.

I kept searching for plausible explanations that might excuse my father's behavior. Unfortunately, the only excuse that I could find pointed to a major problem with drugs. Based on his actions during these trips and everything else I had seen, I had become convinced that he was high most of the time he was with me.

Along with his mood swings, occasionally slurring his words and taking two-hour showers, I noticed his hands seemed to shake most of the time he was with me. As a physician, I knew it wouldn't be too hard for him to get whatever he wanted by simply writing himself a prescription.

In Vegas, I was still trying to figure things out, working to put the clues together about what was wrong with my father. I had convinced myself that once I knew what his problem was, I would be able to save him.

After Vegas, my eyes started to open for the first time. The same question would haunt me late at night as I wondered. *Maybe, my father actually enjoys being "Johnny Russell?" Maybe, I am really seeing him for the first time?*

Every time these questions entered my mind, I immediately suppressed them. I reminded myself that this was my father I was thinking about and not some monster! I began to grasp at anything that would excuse his behavior. I desperately wanted to believe he was a good man and not "Johnny Russell."

There was even a part of me that secretly hoped he did have a pill problem. Drug addiction would allow me to blame all of this on the pills, *and* it meant that he could get help, that he was capable of change.

I know most people would have walked after Vegas. I had been fantasizing about walking away since it started, but I always felt it was my duty to watch his back not just as his son, but as a brother and grandson as well.

However, after Vegas, I wasn't sure I could keep doing it.

Knowing I needed to strengthen my resolve in my mission to protect my family. I wrote down the worst case scenarios for my 79-year-old father before our second trip to Montreal. These were the top five:

"Johnny" having a stroke or heart attack with a prostitute and being found dead in a random brothel.

"Johnny" being shot by an angry pimp for nonpayment or acting out.

"Johnny" being shot by an angry prostitute for nonpayment or acting out.

"Johnny" accidently killing a prostitute while fighting her over a non-payment or non-compliance issue.

"Johnny" dying in a drug-induced psychosis or sex role play situation.

After Vegas, anything was possible.

The more I saw what my father was capable of, even if it was due to a drug induced break from reality, the less power I had to address it. I was devastated emotionally, physically gutted, and yet kept soldiering on denying the reality of the situation I was facing.

Did I blast him for Vegas? Absolutely! Did he apologize and say it would never happen again? Of course! I convinced myself this was what being a man was all about. You did *whatever* it took to protect your family. He also told me things would be different on the next trip.

"Vegas was just a big mistake," he swore. "Let's go back to Montreal. You know how I feel about Patricia, and it will give you a chance to catch up with Alison."

What would have happened if I hadn't been in Vegas to intervene? I often wondered. *What if it got physical and I wasn't there to break it up?*

I convinced myself that I was protecting my family from that Top Five List, and I was protecting my father from himself. Along with my concerns for my grandmother's health and happiness, I was really worried about how my sisters would react to learning the truth about our father.

They had led a sheltered life since they were born and had been valued as his children. While they didn't have a perfect emotional upbringing, they had enjoyed the perks of being children of privilege. They didn't know what it was like to sleep on floors or going a couple of days without food so that you could fix your car.

My childhood had afforded me a much thicker skin and I believed it made me strong enough to see this side of my father. I had always been thankful my sisters never took the hits I did growing up. Ironically, I believed being treated like the bastard son had allowed me to distance myself emotionally from what I was seeing.

I took great pride in the fact that my sisters had chosen low paying jobs that gave back to the community. Unfortunately, I knew they relied heavily on my father and his wife as a way to compensate how little those jobs paid them. From personal shoppers at the finest stores in San Francisco, new cars on their birthdays, and nice houses, they never had to worry about anything financially.

This knowledge had the potential of shattering their perfect lives, and I didn't want them infected with the knowledge that "Johnny Russell" even existed. I also wasn't sure if this wasn't a common practice for men in long-term marriages. My father went to great lengths to legitimize what he was doing with me.

He boasted that most his friends did this on a regular basis, and he mentioned some specific examples. These men were giants in their respective fields and people I had respected. According to my father, all of them were trapped in loveless marriages, and this was just a harmless form of fun.

This was a difficult time for me as a man.

Maybe, I thought, *this was all just some desperate, late-life crisis and the result of a bad marriage. That coupled with a long-term drug problem that I could help him with?* I was desperate to find some type of redeemable quality in him that would explain all of this.

Something I could hold onto...!

Give a desperate person enough time, and they can convince themselves of anything. *I was that desperate.*

During this time, my father started to open up to me in other ways as well.

We talked on the phone every week between our trips, and he had always impressed upon me how important having a son was to him. For the first time, he hinted it wasn't just about furthering the family line. He did it in little ways, like letting me know Michael (his personal trainer) had just had a baby boy.

"Michael's finally got a son," my father tells me in a very solemn voice as if Michael had just joined a special club to which he was a member.

"Good for him," I say sincerely.

"He has been trying and trying to have a boy, but he has only gotten girls up to this point. Three of them!" he says as if the girls were the high price he had to pay for a boy. "Now that he has a son, he can finally stop having children."

"I guess if that's what he was shooting for, I am happy for him," I say, but feel bad for my sisters at that moment. "You know I am so proud of the way Madison and Lisa have turned out. You have obviously done a great job raising them. Look at how they both chose jobs that give back to the community."

"It's nice, but they will never make that much money. I will always have to take care of them financially," my father tells me in a resigned voice. He seems disappointed that I am not getting the message and tries again. "You should have seen how proud Michael was at the gym when he told everyone he finally got a boy from his wife..."

It's conversation like this one that made me believe my father was trying to share something with me or reach out to me in some way and not just using me.

He has to value me. I reasoned with myself whenever I started to question whether he cared about me at all. *I am his only son, and he has told me how important that is to him as a man.*

What I didn't realize at the time was that my father was using this show of favoritism to try and make me feel special so I would continue to enable his behavior. This type of manipulative behavior was something my father had practiced on me my entire life. From day one he carefully crafted his image as the perfect doctor/father.

By the time I was five, I had received lectures about how my father's work as a doctor should allow for a certain amount of latitude when it had come to his conduct as a person. His story has changed over the years, but he has always been the "hero" in it.

When he was an obstetrician, I was told of the countless babies he delivered. How he sacrificed his health and happiness to bring children into this world, day or night. I was told I was selfish in wanting my father to spend time with me, as he brought life into this world. Practicing his profession served a much higher purpose, and I should be proud to have a father that was so selfless.

As I got older and he became an abortionist, I was told stories of what happened to the women who were victims of "back alley" abortions. The horrifying images were burned into my brain as a child; the family told me of the pain and suffering he helped these women avoid. He spent his time doing as many "procedures" as possible because no other doctor was "brave" enough to help these women.

Money was never mentioned as a motive for his career choices, only my father's tireless efforts as a "caregiver/healer."

At this point in my life, the image my father had created for me as a child still clouded my vision. I couldn't quite separate what was real from his highly polished version of things. His marriage was a perfect example of his duplicity. Most people looked at my father's marriage and felt sorry for him. His wife was a shrew, always bossing him around.

When I was fifteen, I remember asking him if he loved Maria. He had just finished telling me the reason he didn't stop her abusive behavior toward me was the effect a divorce would have on my sisters.

I will never forget his simple reply.

"Marriage isn't about love," he said sadly and then continued, "I am doing what's best for the family." I felt pity for him at that moment. I thought if he was willing to sacrifice his happiness and well-being to keep my sisters happy, the least I could do for him was not complain about the verbal abuse I was receiving from his wife.

It was this image that he worked so diligently to create that had convinced me to believe I was missing something, even after what I had witnessed in Vegas. Someone who was so selfless in their actions as both a doctor and father had to be a good man.

Unfortunately, my eyes had not fully opened to who my father really was. I was still desperately clinging to the image my father had created and believed that I was too harsh in my judgment of his actions. I clung to my belief that he was still trapped in an unhappy marriage

He is just looking for someone who will actually love him. I thought. *In Vegas, he was just lashing out at the injustice of how his life turned out. He just needs a little kindness, a little affection. Other than what happened in Vegas, no one is really getting hurt by this....*

I was so desperate to understand my father's thinking; I actually went with this line of thought. As I continued to try my best to rationalize his actions and mine, I decided that I would finally start asking him questions about why he was doing all of this on the next trip.

I just couldn't bring myself to just abandon my father in his time of crisis.

Montreal, Canada: September 1st, 2011

The airport bartender, stewardesses, and even Johnny saw I was on a mission. I had gotten hammered on the flight from Los Angeles to Montreal. I was so drunk that when I get off the plane, I forgot to take my breath mints. Walking down the concourse towards baggage claim my father notices my breath.

"Have you been drinking?" he asks suspiciously as he stops walking toward baggage claim and confronts me.

"No," I say, knowing this is the answer he wants to hear and kicking myself for forgetting the breath mints.

He looks at me for a moment and then smiles. "OK. Then let's go have some fun." We resume our walk to baggage claim. I know he knows I am lying, but calling me on it will interfere with his plans and he seems to be on a mission too. As we walk down the concourse, I start to think about what just happened.

He knows I have been drinking, but really talking about it will ruin his good time, and it obviously isn't worth getting into it for him? I think to my-self as we wait at the baggage carousel. *I guess this is a pretty good indicator about how much he really cares.*

I immediately force this uncomfortable thought from my mind as I grab my carry-on and follow him to the baggage claim.

We catch a cab quickly and settle in for the 30-minute ride into town. I figure this will give us time to catch up on things, but he immediately gets on his burner phone and calls Patricia. I sit silently next to him as he waits for her to pick up the phone.

"Hey babe, I just landed," he says when Patricia answers. "I met David at the airport, and we are going to drop off our bags at the condo before I come over. I should be at Soon's place in about forty minutes."

He talks with her for the rest of the cab ride to the condo, and as we get out of the cab, he finally hangs up the phone.

"Can you take the bags up to the room?" he asks in a tone that sounds more like an order. "The keys should be waiting at the front desk, and I want to get going."

"No problem. Have fun," I tell him while I try to hide my feelings of disappointment.

"Great and call me if there are any problems." he says as he starts walking to the brothel.

I walk up to the front desk and pick up the keys. This is when I realize that I am going to have to drop off a key at the brothel. My stomach turns slightly at the thought of going anywhere near that place as I ride the elevator up to the 12th floor.

*He didn't even want to go to dinner...*I think to myself sadly as the elevator hits the 12th floor and then I chastise myself for being so weak. *Stop being a child! This is just the way the world works...*

As I walk into the luxury condo, a huge mirror faces the entrance, and I glance at my reflection, but quickly look down. I am starting to realize that I am just a means to an end to my father. I am embarrassed that it bothers me so much and get angry with myself. I drop off our bags inside. I decide to drop off his key as soon as possible and slam the door shut.

At least I might get to see Alison. I tell myself as I try and look for the bright side in all of this. *She seems to like hanging out with me and maybe she has forgotten about the text.*

Before dropping off the key at the brothel, I stop at a local bar for a little liquid courage. After two shots of straight Vodka, my nerves settle, and I relax for a second. I text Johnny, letting him know I will leave his key with Soon if he is busy. Unfortunately, my father has other plans.

"David, how have you been?" Soon greets me warmly the moment I open the door to the brothel. As hammered as I am right now, I still feel incredibly uneasy in this place; I can't wait to get out of here.

"Doing fine, Soon, I just came to drop off Johnny's key with you," I say quickly, fumbling my words together.

"Why don't you stay a while? Johnny said he would pay for any of the girls if you want to get a massage," Soon says hopefully.

"Uh, that's ok. I just came to drop off the key," I say quickly as I try and hand it to her.

"No, No. Johnny asked me to get him when you came." Soon tells me.

"That's really okay. No need to disturb him, here is the key," I say desperately trying to give her the key, but she has already started walking down the hallway toward the back of the place. A moment later my father appears, and he is in the process of buttoning up his jeans. His hair is a wreck, and he is sweating profusely as if he just stopped whatever he was doing a couple of seconds ago.

"Are you sure you don't want to get a massage before you see Alison?" my father asks me in a hopeful tone.

"No thanks. Here is the key. I am going to surprise Alison," I say quickly and practically sprint out of the place.

As I walk outside the building that houses the brothel, I decide to have a couple more shots before I go to the strip club. I need to get my blood pressure back to a normal level and being in the brothel again has just freaked me out.

You are being weak; I think to myself angrily as I down my first shot. *You are beating yourself up for nothing and being too sensitive. You just need to learn how to relax and enjoy yourself!*

I am completely hammered by the time I finally walk into the strip club. Alison literally screams, "David!!!" and then runs across the club and wraps her arms around me. One of the bouncers gives me a look and then smiles. Her reaction is a rare display of public affection that is generally frowned upon in strip clubs, but he seems to understand the situation better than I do.

A wave of emotion hits me as I realize how much I have missed her, and I am choked up by the fact she obviously missed me too. She wastes no time in telling me she lost her cell phone my last night there. When she found it, she had tried calling me several times, but I never picked up.

She actually cares about me, I think to myself at the moment, *she isn't just acting!*

In that moment of weakness and confusion, I decide to stop being so noble. Maybe this is just the way the world works....

Alison immediately suggests we go back to my place and bring her friend with us for a private dance. I agree quickly as I down my second cape cod, but I really just want to be alone with her. The warmth from all of the alcohol in me is radiating through my body, and that along with my increasing need to connect with someone overwhelms my sense of right and wrong.

I decide to embrace what I had resisted for so long.

This is my first experience with two women, and I wish I could say it is something special, but I can't. I know what I am doing is wrong the second I start and while I "perform," there is no connection during the physical act. There is an instant sense of shame and regret the moment we are done.

No matter how much I try to rationalize what I have done, I can't hide from the fact that I know this whole thing is wrong. Whatever my father may think of me, I know I am a better man than this. I lie in bed hating myself for compromising my integrity, yet again.

As hard as I tried to be my father's son, at that moment, I realize that I just wasn't "that guy."

As dawn approaches, Alison's friend tries to wake her up and get her out of bed. I can tell Alison wants to stay because she is pretending to be in a dead sleep. Her friend is having none of it and starts speaking to her in French.

"Get out of bed, Alison, we have to go, and you don't know if he really wants you to stay!" her friend says sternly, not realizing I speak a little French.

"I just want to stay here and see what it is like to wake up with him. Just leave me!" Alison replies sleepily as she pulls the sheets even tighter around her.

I tell her friend I am fine with her spending the night, but she won't back down. Eventually, they leave, and I tell Alison I will meet her at the club later. As I shut the door to the condo, I wonder how many others were out there like them. Women who are afraid to spend the night because of what they do for a living.

The whole thing is sad and hollow.

Hours later, my "brother" and his "girlfriend" Patricia greet me like a conquering hero. Patricia goes on and on about how we woke them up last night and how it sounded like we were having a great time. I am the opposite of happy; I feel like I not only let myself down but Alison as well.

I had wanted to do the right thing by Alison, and I know I have failed.

My "brother" is especially proud of me. Not because I scored a touchdown, ran my own business or found the right women to settle down with. Not because I worked hard, achieved something meaningful or did something honorable. His pride was derived from the fact I had a three way.

At that moment, I realized: I will never be like "Johnny Russell." This is a truth that I know I have to hold onto with both hands now.

Patricia, it turns out, has decided to stay with us at the condo. I later find out she made this decision only because she feels safer with me around. Sadly, I have a new value to my father beyond that of a beard; I represent safety to the other girls.

"Johnny" is adding the "girlfriend" experience to his repertoire and being a "boyfriend" is a new part of his act. He can be seen in public with them now, and they feel comfortable being alone with him, as long as I was nearby. Patricia's friends had warned her about his dark side and that he had a hard time taking no for an answer when he wanted to try something new.

My "brother" is having a blast with Patricia, who was working her way through nursing school. I can tell Patricia has fallen for "Johnny's" act, but he tells me, "I am going to take my time with Patricia." He has just broken up with one of his other girls, Xian, a young woman from China who didn't speak a lot of English.

He brags to me that she is inconsolable since he broke it off and that the Soon is very upset with him for breaking her heart. I can hear the pride in his voice when he says, "They can't even say my name at the brothel without her bursting into tears."

When I hear this, I realize how far my father has fallen from the man I thought I knew. I know it is time for me to try and help my father see the error of his ways. I can't put it off anymore; I need to get to the bottom of why he is doing this. I start asking my father questions the following day.

It is our third day here, and we are walking toward the Natural History Museum. Patricia is at school, so my father has a break in his schedule, and I mention it would be nice to take a walk around town. I secretly hope I will get some insight into his behavior and get up my courage to ask him a question that has been on my mind since this started.

"Did Grandpa ever do this type of stuff with you?"

"Of course not!" he replies angrily. "This is something I figured out on my own!"

His anger at the question makes me pause for a moment. I don't want to piss him off, but I have to figure out why he goes to such great lengths to play this game with women. But I need more information, so I can start to help him. Obviously, I have to be careful about how I approach him, but I have a million questions.

Was he punishing some woman from his past? I wonder. *Fighting feelings of powerlessness? What was really going on here?*

As we walk inside the Natural History Museum, I build up the courage to ask another question.

"Is everything alright with your health, you are not dying or anything, are you?" I ask.

"I am fine. I am actually in a lot better shape than you are," he says with judgment in his voice. "Why are you asking me all of these questions?"

"I am just trying to figure out why you decided to share this with me after all of these years," I tell him honestly.

"I just thought it would be fun," he says as we walk through the botanical garden now. "It's just a way to spend a little quality father/son time together and blow off some steam."

It turns out he has an agenda for our walk as well and before I can get to my next question he asks, "You and Alison seem to be getting along pretty good now, right?"

"I guess so. We're just seeing what happens," I reply quickly, and I am now instantly on guard.

"What you need to do is what I do," he tells me smugly, "get her to fall in love with you so she won't charge you anymore. See her for a while and once you get bored, just dump her."

In those couple of sentences my father manages to decimate any respect I have left for him. Hearing how he really feels about these women is like getting sucker punched. I am a little dazed. I finally get a glimpse of who my father truly is at his core, but as sick as it makes me, I know I can't let him see how disgusted I am.

"I don't know how I feel about her at this point. I guess we'll see what happens as things progress," I reply as I am now starting to regret trying to find out why he is doing this.

Some things you just can't un-hear.

"I wonder what the girls lives are like when we aren't there," I say, trying to evoke some kind of compassion out of him. I hope he will think for a second about how depressing their lives must be.

"It's not much of a life," he says with clinical detachment. "They work all the time when they're there but make good money. They just keep looking for Mr. Right."

"Seems kind of sad, doesn't it?" I ask, hoping for some emotional response.

"No. You just have to convince them you are Mr. Right!" he replies brightly. We walk the rest of the way in silence. I just don't want to hear anymore.

After that walk in the park, the guilt I feel for participating in what my father was doing increased dramatically. It wasn't just the morality of it. These women were just trying to make a living and find someone to love them. They didn't deserve this type of mental manipulation.

If anything, they deserved a little kindness.

The guilt came out in my night terrors. To combat them and my nagging conscience, I had started drinking even heavier on this trip. I went from tying one on at night to Bloody Marys for breakfast. Even with the amount of alcohol I was consuming and the sleep medication I was on, the night terrors were making a regular appearance.

The next day during breakfast, I get that look from Patricia, the same one my friend Alex and Matt gave me in Los Angeles. It is obvious she has heard one of my "night terrors" last night, and she finally works up her courage to ask me about them.

"Your brother told me about your nightmares, but I wasn't prepared for last night," she says sweetly, and I immediately tell her I am sorry if I woke her.

"It sounded like someone was trying to kill you, but when I turned over, I saw Johnny sound asleep!" Patricia continues with that same look of pity in her eyes. "I decided it was best for me not to wake you."

"It's no big deal; he has been having them since he was a kid," my father interjects, and then shoots me an annoyed look as if to ask, "*Are you trying to screw up my good time?*"

My relationship with Alison was also beginning to irritate "Johnny." I am straying from the script and not following his standard operating procedure, in fact, I am doing the exact opposite. He can tell I am starting to develop feelings for her and not subjecting her to *his* idea of a good time.

Although I knew I screwed up by sleeping with her, I was determined to show her that there was such a thing as a good man. I knew she has seen some terrible examples of what men were capable of, and I wanted to demonstrate by my actions, that I valued who she was inside and that she wasn't just a sex object.

Alison had started to open up to me the day before my walk in the park with my father.

"I actually read the text you had sent me before you left last time," she said quietly. "I didn't lose my phone. I called you several times the day you left, but you never picked up the phone."

My mind flashed to my burner phone ringing in the airport trash can as she continues, "I wanted to answer your text, but it was too difficult for me. A lot of guys want to save me, but I never met one I wanted to be saved by ... before you."

I assured her that the offer still stood. But Alison shook her head. "It's too late now. I have accepted that this is my life, and I don't want to go back to the cubical world."

As much as I tried to hide my feelings for Alison, once my father saw them, he decided to put a stop to the relationship. Like he always does, he used his money to make his point.

We started going to some high-end restaurants that made Alison very uncomfortable. She came from a humble background, and he knew it. She was very careful not to embarrass herself in front of everyone, but still he enjoyed her obvious discomfort.

It was like scenes straight out of *Pretty Woman*, and it would have been endearing if I hadn't felt so bad for her. But every time I asked her if she was enjoying herself, she told me, "Of course I am."

On our last night out in Montreal, my suspicions were confirmed about my father's drug use. We were on our way to dinner when he got out of our cab, and a bunch of pills fell out of his pocket and onto the seat. While I have always suspected he was on something during our trips, I thought it was just recreational until Vegas. As I looked down at the seat, I was shocked at how many different sizes and colors of pills were on the seat. I scooped them up and gave them to him.

He took them without saying a word.

Even though an entire pharmacy had just spilled out of his pocket, I didn't say a word about it. I was afraid of what he might say, and I had seen too much of "Johnny" on this trip.

After dinner, that night, Alison and I walk back to my place. As we pass some drunken sorority girls, one of them stumbles in front of us and almost falls. I catch her and then hand her off to her friends. Alison tried to make it less awkward for her.

"I have the same problem when I drink and wear high heels," she says kindly, but the drunken girl takes it the wrong way.

"Maybe I'm not wearing a silk dress from Neiman's," the girl sneers, "but at least I don't do what you do to get it."

"You had better take your friend home NOW!" I tell the girls angrily as I try and control my rage. "AND teach her some manners while you are at it!!!"

They quickly apologize and carry their friend away from us.

As we continue to walk toward the condo, Alison gets upset and starts to cry. "I wasn't making fun of her! I just wanted her to feel better and not be embarrassed," she says to me in a voice so sincere it breaks my heart a little.

I don't know how she guessed Alison was a stripper. Maybe it was her accent, but Alison is deeply upset. It reminds me she is just a kind soul who treated everyone she met with kindness and compassion. The drunken girl had hurt her simply to prove that she was superior in her mind, and it really bothers me.

Would my sisters have made a similar comment? I wonder. *They have never known any hardship or what it is like to truly be on their own.*

During this time, I had been thinking about my sisters a lot and wondered how my father could sleep with women younger than his daughters and treat them so horribly. How could the father of two young women act like "Johnny Russell," showing no empathy for the plight these women suffered?

Was their lack of money, education and social status, the only thing that separated these women from his daughters in his mind? I wondered as I got ready for bed that night.

The more I look at what my father is doing, the more his whole life seems like a lie. Everything was an empty gesture, a posturing action with an ulterior motive. It took going through this experience to make me start to tear apart his carefully crafted image and start judging him based on his actions.

What kind of a person uses women the way he does? I couldn't help wondering. *Throwing them away like used printer cartridges!*

That night, I finally stopped turning a blind eye to what my father was doing, and I realized that I had had it backward all this time: I didn't have a decent man for a father who sometimes, in faraway places, acted like the sleazebag Johnny Russell.

Johnny Russell *was* my father.

CHAPTER FIVE

THE DIVORCE

Over the course of four trips, my father's carefully crafted image melted in front of my eyes, and he became "Johnny Russell." Every excuse I tried to find for his behavior uncovered something more horrifying.

My reaction? *I tried drinking myself into oblivion.*

In my more sober moments, I was still engaging in all kinds of mental and moral contortions when the truth was I didn't want to – I couldn't – face the fact that "Johnny" was my father. I didn't want to accept that I came from someone who was capable of such cruelty.

Did he see himself in me? I wondered as my thoughts grew darker. *Was this the reason he shared this dark secret with me?*

Ironically, the only hope I still carried for my father's soul came in the form of Patricia. He seemed to genuinely care for her, and I noticed a change in his behavior. He treated her with a type of respect that he hadn't used with the other "girlfriends."

She was trying to make a better life for herself by studying to be a nurse, and he seemed to respect her. They often talked about medicine, and I secretly hoped she would help humanize these women in his eyes. My hope seemed to have merit. For the year and a half that they had seen each other, he had only been attentive, kind and loving to Patricia the entire time.

Maybe she could serve as a beacon of hope to my father, I desperately clung to this thought, *A ray of light in the otherwise dark and depressing world that was consuming him.*

When he was around her, I saw glimpses of my old father, or the man I was raised to believe in: a kind man who cared for others.

I knew I wasn't going to be able to help my father at this point. He didn't want it. Every time I tried to bring up the subject of morals, consequences or basic human decency, he immediately shut me down.

So Patricia, the one I began to think of as the younger, nicer version of Maria, became my last hope for saving my father's humanity. I began to fantasize about how she would inspire him to make some good choices and not continue down this dark path. Most importantly, I hoped she would teach him to be compassionate and caring toward others.

The preparation for the trips themselves always started with the same routine.

First, I would call my Grandma, telling her I was going on a trip with my father and hearing her happiness. By this time, however, even the sound of her voice failed to bring me any satisfaction. I had *never* lied to my grandmother. But now, her obvious happiness was based on a lie, and

I felt like I didn't deserve to talk to her anymore.

Ironically, by protecting her, I had become unworthy of my grandmother in my mind.

It wasn't just my grandmother either. I found myself constantly lying to friends and colleagues about what I was doing on these trips, even though the effect they had on me was visible to everyone. One of my friends and clients Scott finally called me on it.

Drunk, I had sent him an email at 2 am before leaving on the trip to Cancun. In it, I asked him to email my stepfather if something happened to me while I was on this trip. I wanted to let my grandmother know I wasn't like "Johnny Russell." Scott called me the following morning when I was at the airport, and he wasted no time in telling me what he thought.

"Hey buddy, I got your email from last night," Scott tells me as soon as I answer the phone and puts my mind at ease immediately. "If things go bad, I will handle it. You don't have to worry about that."

"Thanks, I really appreciate it," I say and start to feel a little bit better. I had been having second thoughts about sending the email all morning. "I know it is a weird favor to ask you for, but I didn't know who I could trust with the email."

"Don't worry about it, but I have to tell you I am worried about you," Scott says in a rare display of emotion. "I talked with my wife last night, and we both think your father is just using you. I know you won't tell me what is happening on these trips, but each time you take one, it seems to really screw you up."

"I am just doing what I think is right buddy," I say trying to get off the subject. "Please tell your wife I said thanks for worrying about me, but I can handle it."

"That's why you sent me a death email at 2 am, right?" he asks sarcastically. Scott always says what he is thinking, and we have been extremely blunt with each other over the years. We have also talked about our fathers and our less than perfect childhoods. I think he understands what I am going through because he went through something far worse than what I am experiencing.

His stepfather had beaten him so severely when he was a kid that he spent two months in the hospital. That and only being able to see the color blue out of one eye was the price he was willing to pay to protect his mother. He naturally understands my reluctance to get into details with him about the trips with my father. Some things you just don't want to talk about, but he also knows the risks of doing the right thing as well.

In my mind, he is a hero and has paid a far greater price for protecting his family than I am.....

"I don't think anything will happen on this trip," I say calmly and put my manager voice on. "I am just covering all my bases just in case. I am sure everything will go smoothly."

As I hang up the phone, I think about what a good friend I have in Scott. He is a good human being all the way through and his actions prove it every day. Not only is he a brilliant artist, but he didn't follow the path of his violent stepfather. He raised his son as a single father and never touched him.

Recently, he adopted another son who came from a similar family background. He was reversing the cycle of abuse he had come from by stepping up to the plate like a man. I had asked Scott if I could wire him extra money for gifts for his adopted son. Scott had always done well financially, but he knew I wanted his son to know there were other people that cared about him as well.

The moment I hang up, Scott sends me a picture of his adopted son with a skateboard I had just bought him. I email him back a thank you as we pulled away from the jetway and tell him it was nice to know there are still good people out there.

Looking back on it now, I realize I was subconsciously trying to associate myself with a healthy male role model/father figure in my friendship with Scott.

Cancun, Mexico: January 19th, 2012

The trip to Cancun was the same as the rest of them, and they were mechanical in nature at this point.

We always flew in a couple of hours before his "girlfriend" got there. The first thing I would do is go through his luggage to make sure there was no identifying information anywhere his girlfriend would have access to and then locked up his suitcase. I double checked everything and often found stuff he missed.

This trip, as I was going over my father's stuff, I began to hope this would be the last time I would have to do this. My father seemed pretty serious about Patricia. Maybe he would just make her his permanent girl and not have to keep going to the brothels. I could just say I was with him and wouldn't have to actually participate in the "vacation" itself.

This wasn't as farfetched as it sounded.

My father had asked Cindy in Vegas how much his previous girl Xian had made per year working for Soon. He had balked at the figure (about 120 grand), but maybe Patricia wasn't as expensive. He seemed open to having someone in Texas now, and I was really hoping this might get me off the hook for the trips.

Further, since Maria didn't seem to mind, I figured he could just keep a mistress on the side in Texas. Maybe this would allow us to go back to being father and son.

Maybe...

After I finish my father's luggage search, I realize he has been pacing around the room and is starting to act a little manic. I know he is upset about something, and I make the mistake of asking him what's up.

"Patricia is late. She should have been here an hour ago," my father replies angrily.

"Are you sure?" I ask and then try to calm him down. "Maybe she just got hung up at customs."

"Her plane landed two hours ago, I checked already," he says bitterly, and he starts to get really worked up. "My whole trip is going to be ruined if she is a no show! How could she do this to me!! What am I going to do now?"

"I am sure she is on her way," I say weakly. Apparently the thought of spending this trip with just me is a very unpleasant notion to my father, and this really hits me hard.

"Or she just decided to keep the money I sent her for the ticket and not come," he spits back. He either doesn't realize or maybe even care that what he is saying is having a brutal effect on me.

"Give it a little more time before you get upset," I say as the alcohol in my system feels like it has evaporated. I feel like my nerves are raw right now and have a strong desire to numb out. "I am going to go back to my room to lie down for a little bit. I think I have jet lag. I am sure she will be here soon."

"Fine, I will let you know if she shows up," he says in a dismissive tone.

Once I get back to my room, I open up my suitcase. After Vegas, I stopped unpacking when I traveled, and I was always ready to go at a moment's notice. It takes me a moment to find the large vodka bottle I had stashed for this trip. I crack the seal as I grab it by the neck and take a 10-second pull that makes my eyes water.

I wait for the warm glow of the alcohol to fill my body, but I feel nothing. I had begun to rely heavily on my best friend Vodka to get me through these trips. It usually fogged things up enough that I didn't have to really look at the circumstances, my father's character or myself. Unfortunately, my best friend was no longer working.

Despite all my efforts, I saw everything with crystal clear focus now.

I get a call from my father 40 minutes later. It turns out that Patricia had taken a bus from the airport instead of a cab, and that was the reason she was late. Patricia was always trying to impress my father with how careful she was with his money. She had been around him long enough to see how important the almighty dollar was to him.

That night, we went to a romantic dinner, just the three of us. My father had the Mariachi band serenade Patricia several times; she looked entranced. The entire scene was an eerie echo of the 60th birthday party my father threw for his wife. They invited about 150 high-profile people from Texas, and my father had a 15-piece mariachi band serenade Maria several times.

I imagine Maria had the same reaction as Patricia, but I can't say this with total certainty. It was difficult to see her as I wasn't sitting at the family table. I had been seated at the servants' table toward the back of the room.

While alcohol had started to fail me in this trip, I get lost in that moment when "Johnny" complains about the fact I have ordered flan for dessert.

"You know that isn't going to help your cholesterol, especially since you are already overweight," he says in a judgmental tone I am very familiar with.

"Dad, I am fine, the last time I got it checked, my cholesterol was actually below normal."

"Dad?" Patricia asks somewhat confused.

SHIT!!!! I think to myself as I look over and see a rage in my father's eyes I have never seen before. I cover as quick as I can.

"That's what I call him sometimes when he acts more like a dad than a brother," I explain quickly, but I see my father is about to explode, so I continue. "He is always treating me like a son instead of a brother since he basically raised me himself. It gets a little annoying at times, and this is the only way I can stop him from doing it."

Patricia smiles as she looks at me and says, "That's sweet. Do you think he will ever stop?"

"I don't know," I say, as I try and change the subject. "He has his days. Some days I am his son and then some days I am his brother. Do you have any brothers or sisters?"

"No, I am an only child," she says sadly, but brightens as she looks at my father. "But I am hoping to start my own family, and I want lots of children."

My father looks at her and smiles. Then he looks at me and his face changes. He gives me the same look he uses when he is about to drop the hammer on one of his "girlfriends."

Later that night, I ask my father if I can talk to him alone for a moment when we are in the hotel lobby. He glares at me and then asks Patricia to go up to the room.

"I will be up in a minute, why don't you take a bath and get ready for me," he tells her as he gives her a quick kiss.

At that moment, I was really angry with myself for slipping. I had been beating myself up mentally since it happened and I couldn't get it out of my mind.

"I am so sorry. It just slipped out," I say apologetically, the moment she gets on the elevator.

"How could you be so stupid, WHAT were you thinking!" my father shouts loudly, and I realize the lobby may not have been the best place to apologize. I start to stammer.

"I am really-"

"Thoughtless? Selfish?" he practically screams. "Do you have any idea of the questions I am going to be asked when I get up to that room?"

"I am sorry. I have been so careful. I think she bought the excuse," I say desperately; I know I screwed up, and it is killing me. "I-"

"STOP. The damage is done, and now I have to fix it. Just try using your brain for once!" he says and then he storms off toward the elevator.

I look around, and I see the staff has been watching, but they quickly look away.

It didn't occur to me that I was the one who should have been pissed off for being forced to pretend I wasn't his son. Things were so screwed up at that point; I felt I had somehow let him down. In the year and a half since this started, I didn't realize that I had been taught that calling my father "Dad," was wrong.

By breakfast the next morning, I knew things were going downhill. He is starting to play the same game with Patricia that he had with Cindy in Vegas. He has turned off the affection mixed with attentiveness and turned on an attitude of indifference and contempt. I am hoping my slip up the night before wasn't the reason for my father's change of heart. I really like Patricia.

We are cruising toward the Marriage part of "The Experience," and my eyes are now open to what is really happening. My father's promise to "take his time with her," takes on a new and cruel meaning as I under-stand this – a drawn-out romance and then a vicious breakup – has been his plan all along.

Every time I look at "Johnny" and Patricia, I see the lie, the deceit.

Patricia's honest love for my father and his fake affection for her is a painful, but stark reminder of my relationship with him. It was getting to the point where I just want to scream at her, "He doesn't love you, he is just using you, and you will never be anything more than a *whore* to him!!"

I should have been shouting at a mirror.

After my screw up at dinner, my father wouldn't even look at me. His anger at me magnified the situation I was in until I could no longer ignore it. As we rode the bus to the Xplore water park the following day, I couldn't stop thinking about it and kept coming to the same conclusion: he considers you a whore, not a son. Because you have allowed him to pay for the trips, he thinks he has bought you – your time, your allegiance, your help, your conscience.

I am on the clock, just like Patricia.

Of course, he never paid me – had he offered, I would have knocked his teeth out – but the room, plane tickets, and food were all on him and Maria. I would have gladly paid both of them *not to go,* but that wasn't the deal, and we all knew it.

"*You're nothing but a whore to him,*" I kept telling myself quietly over and over in the bus. I knew very well how he treated whores.

It turns out the water park has these little gas powered cars you ride around to explore the underground caves and wildlife. The track is about four and a half miles long. Something inside of me snaps. I decide I am going to run through it like the hammers of hell.

"Johnny" sits in the passenger seat and Patricia in back, once they let us go, I won't stop. I race full speed ahead. I want to escape this feeling of powerlessness, and I still have a small hope my father might fear for our safety. I almost flip the car three times, and I still don't know how I didn't run it off the rope bridge.

Not once does "Johnny" try to stop me.

"Please stop, David! I don't want to die!" Patricia finally cries out. That's what gets me to stop. While I have no problem risking my life or "Johnny's," I remember that Patricia is an innocent in all of this.

By the time the park employees catch up with us, they are beyond pissed ... and they have every right to be. We are escorted off the track and asked not to ride the ride again, ever.

After that, Patricia and "Johnny" spent more alone time together in their room. Whether he was aware that I didn't want to participate in his latest game or that I was starting to wake up to the fact he was using me, I will never know. Patricia thought he was being romantic, but I knew the bitter truth: he was getting everything he could in before the Divorce.

I was starting to realize that my father didn't believe in any of the things he had taught me as a child. The emphasis on family loyalty at the expense of oneself was solely for "his" benefit. Everything he taught me wasn't to prepare for life; it was to *exploit* me and get *him* what he wanted. Of course, thinking like this was very new to me and I was battling decades of programming.

It would take a couple of years for me to come to terms with the extent of emotional manipulation and abuse I had been subjected to, under the guise of as life lessons and tough love.

Looking back on it now I realize that my father and Maria offered me no love, no concern, no pride, no care, no real emotional investment. From day one, I had been groomed for my position as his brother/beard/ cleaner. When my father looked at me, even when I was a young adult, he didn't see a person or a son. He saw a potential fall guy, a beard and when I was young, he saw me as a cute kid who could act as bait and get him laid.

When a parent behaves that way toward his child, some of it is always internalized. I was no exception. My whole life, I suspected that he didn't love me simply because I was unlovable. Like Patricia, my need to be loved made it easier for my father to manipulate me. When my eyes finally started to open up to the fact that my father wasn't only manipulating Patricia but me as well, I dove deeper into my denial and drinking.

It's a tough thing when the person you've been raised to respect turns out to be a total fraud as a human being. It gets worse when you come to the painful conclusion that he has been using you. I had stuck with it this long because I was desperate to find some redeeming quality in my father, even some way I might save him.

It was like trying to help someone swimming in a sewer, and enjoying it; as I tried to pull him out, he yanked me in with him.

Patricia's plight really started to disturb me as the trip wore on. The more I saw how she genuinely cared about my father, the more disgusted I became with his behavior. I'm sure she got some money, but not anywhere near what she should have. The fact that he was getting a deal was part of the fun for him!

She was young, pretty and full of hope. She was a little different than the others. For example, she insisted "Johnny" tip the maids every day and tried to save him money by taking the bus. I liked her for all the reasons I didn't like "Johnny." She was a good human being, just looking for love.

But like so many others, she had taken the bait and bought into the story of "Johnny Russell," hook, line, and sinker. She saw in him a hard-working, selfless person. And she thought he loved her. She had talked about how important family was to her and hoped one day to have a family of her own. She hadn't met the man behind the mask. She hadn't even suspected he existed.

Knowing how this story was going to end, I couldn't bear to watch it again.

At the end of the trip, I checked out early and went to look for a cab to take me to the airport. I had managed to make it through another "vacation," and I couldn't wait to get out of there. That's when I found Patricia sitting in front of the hotel, sobbing. When I left their room an hour before to say goodbye, things between them seemed tense, but civil. I sat down next to her and asked what happened.

I had known the answer before she told me, but I wanted to give her a chance to let it out. Because they had been "seeing" each other for so long, "Johnny" had the chance to set the hooks in deep. When he ripped them out, in his usual brutal way, he tore out a part of her with it, causing maximum damage.

I will never understand why he enjoyed hurting women this way, but it was the only thing that seemed to make him happy.

He knew he had been her white knight in shining armor, the one she could always think of as good in her life. He worked very hard to get her to believe in him and to emotionally invest in the idea of their future together. He was her hope, a man she loved and was devoted to the idea of building a future together. Now he got to take it all away from her. He had the pleasure of proving to her this whole time; she had been nothing more than a *whore* to him.

No one deserves that type of cruelty.

I sat with her for about 30 minutes and listened to the whole story. They were going to get married. He was going to settle down in the States; she had convinced him he had done enough for the poor women in war-torn Afghanistan. They were going to start a family. In that last hour in their room, he just changed. It was as if a switch was flipped on his personality. Once his bags were packed, he said it was over, and that was it.

She had begged and pleaded. "If you want to continue your work in Afghanistan, that's alright with me!"

It made no difference to him. "I am looking out for what's best for you!" he told her. "I'm just looking for a girlfriend."

"I'm just looking for a girlfriend." That's when it hit me; I bet he never even went to Afghanistan. I ask Patricia if she needs anything.

"No," she says. "I'm just waiting for the bus to take me to the airport." I tell her I think "Johnny" has made a huge mistake, and quite frankly I am sick of his behavior. Patricia looks at me with compassion. "I know. I could always see it in your eyes. Take care of yourself."

This lady has just been emotionally destroyed, and she is worried about *me...*?

On the flight home, I thought a lot about my life, "Johnny Russell," and the women we hurt. I say "we" because I was enabling him at this point and I knew it. I decided I couldn't be a part of his cruelty anymore; I was done no matter what the cost. Two weeks after our trip, I called him to let him know I don't want to be a part of it anymore.

"Hey, Dad."

"Hello, Son. I have to tell you I had a great time in Cancun, and I am really looking forward to our next trip!" he says happily.

"About that, I was thinking-," I say as I try to start my speech about getting out, but he interrupts me.

"You know it really means the world to me that I get to share this with you," he says, and I quickly realize he suspects I am going to end the trips as he continues. "It's like we are finally getting to connect as father and son. I know you pulled away from the family because of your difficulties with Maria, but now we get to spend time together, just you and me."

"Dad, I really enjoy spending time with you and-"

"I know you have been angry with me for not sticking up for you with Maria." My father interrupts me again trying to avoid what is coming, "I have always tried to do what is best for the family, and divorcing Maria would have destroyed your sisters."

"Dad, that was a long time ago, I am really calling to talk to you about something else." I say very quickly, so he can't interrupt me as I press ahead, "It is about the trips!"

"What is it, son?" my father asks, but the tone of his voice has changed slightly. He is now on guard. I know I can't stop now, so I bite the bullet.

"I am happy to take the trips with you, and I enjoy spending time with you, but do we have to bring other people with us all the time?" I ask. There is a minute pause before my father replies.

"What is this really about, David?" he asks. "I know the last couple of trips haven't been perfect, but I have been trying to establish a better relationship with you. Don't you want to have a closer relationship?"

"Of course, I want a closer relationship," I say, and I can tell he is gearing up for a fight. "That's the whole reason I have been going on the tr-"

"I have to go. I have a patient waiting for me," my father interrupts me and says, "Let's talk about this in a week or so when you have a chance to calm down."

"Dad, I am not upset, I just want to talk about some things," I say calmly.

"Fine. Let's talk next week; we have plenty of time," he says. "I love you, David."

"I love you too, dad," I say, but I can tell he has already hung up the phone.

The next week we talked and I asked him if there was any way we could go back to being father and son. He said he was happy to discuss it, but he wanted to do it in person and not over the phone. Could we just meet in Vegas, sit down and hash things out?

With great reluctance, I finally agreed.

Las Vegas, Nevada: April 13th, 2012

In Vegas, this time, "Johnny" was on his best behavior with his new girlfriend, Pam. I was surprised he had brought another "girlfriend" on the trip, but I guess this was his idea of sitting down and hashing out my deep discomfort with the whole thing. He made it very clear to me that I was being unreasonable with my reluctance to participate in a little harmless fun.

In short, it was his way or the highway.

I stayed drunk the entire trip; morning, noon and night I was completely hammered. I couldn't face the fact that the only value my father really placed on me was that of his brother/beard/cleaner.

This time, "Johnny Russell" didn't get the hopeful hooker wanting to be loved. This one, Pam, was all business. She was there to do a job, not fall in love. This was a small relief. Seeing those other women stare at him with adoring eyes, only to see them broken-hearted once he was done with them had become too much for me.

This trip to Vegas, there was no honeymoon, and there was no marriage, so there was no divorce. No fights, no breakup, no crying. Everyone left happy ...but "Johnny."

I saw he was just going through the motions. He had nothing to look forward to, no punishment to dole out. He hadn't gotten the thrill of inflicting tremendous pain on someone. No one suffered because of his sadistic games.

At first, I was relieved to be spared the sight. But then I wondered, *what is he going to do next?* He seemed to really get off on pushing things as far as he possibly could. Somehow he felt the lines of basic human decency and kindness didn't apply to him. He thought he was above it all because of his money, profession and social position in life.

Now I was terrified of what he might be willing to do next to revisit that thrill, and how he might expect me to help him.

My head was spinning. I wasn't sleeping. The drinking wasn't helping. My work was suffering. I was miserable in every way. I realized I needed to talk with someone.

I needed to talk to a professional.

CHAPTER SIX

PROFESSIONAL HELP

Margaret was the first person I talked to about "Johnny Russell." I hadn't spoken to her in 20 years, but I knew she was a kind soul, and I knew I needed professional help!

In trying to manage things on my own, I had painted myself into a corner, and I saw no other way out. I needed to talk with someone who had experience with dealing with this type of situation. Hiding from my problems in a bottle wasn't working, and it was time for me to face them head on.

Margaret had been my therapist in Los Angeles when I was a kid going through the custody battle between my parents. Not only was she a good person, but she knew my back story. She has been a therapist for 35 years, on staff at several teaching hospitals including, UCLA.

I was sure Margaret had dealt with something like this before...

Given our history, I was comfortable with Margaret. She was sixty-three now, but her tendency to be brutally honest had not faded with time. While I was ashamed of what I had done with "Johnny," I told her everything in our first session. The first question I asked her was the one that had been plaguing me since this started.

"Please tell me this is something you have heard of?"

I believe she saw hope in my eyes, but she wouldn't lie. She gave me the same look I'd received before from Alex, Matt, and Patricia: pity mixed with shock. "I'm sorry, David, but I haven't heard of this type of behavior before."

Apparently, this doesn't happen all the time. This doesn't happen – period.

You have to really swing for the fences for a therapist with 35 years experience to not even have *heard* of something like this. Whatever hope I had inside me that this was even a semi-normal thing died at that moment.

As I began to tell Margaret about the trips with my father and the emotional fallout, I thought about the advice I would have given a client facing this situation.

Ironically, if a client told me about the situation with my father, my advice would have been the exact opposite of what I had actually done. I would have told the client that family loyalty is admirable, but it can also blind you to the obvious. And if it's misplaced, it can do real damage. Margaret's insight clarified for me what I am sure is painfully obvious to the outside observer: I was being used.

In business, I would have caught this in an instant.

I've known for decades that in business, a person's actions, not his or her words, dictate how they really feel. Everyone talks a good game in Hollywood, and compliments fly in every direction. But if you really want to see how they feel about you, wait until you see the deal itself. Actions, not words are what really matter in Hollywood. The same philosophy applies to family too, but my need for my father's love (someone universally acknowledged to be looking out for their children) made me an easy target to manipulate.

Had this been a business deal, I would have ended it at the first trip. Unfortunately, this was family (At least for me) and that had blinded me. After hearing everything, Margaret gave me some insight into what she thought was wrong with my father at the end of our first session.

"It sounds like he is suffering from an extreme case of Narcissistic Personality Disorder," she suggested. "While I don't like to diagnosis someone I haven't met with, it is almost a textbook case from the symptoms you have described. This isn't only abnormal behavior, but it shows a level of acting out that is simply off the charts and dangerous."

"Are you sure he isn't just a sex addict with a massive drug problem?" I ask hopefully. I knew I could help him with an addiction issue.

"He may be afflicted with those diseases as well, but this pattern of behavior suggests you are dealing with an extreme Narcissistic Personality, which has obviously been left unchecked for decades."

"What about his friends?" I ask, as I unknowingly start my routine of defending him. "He told me that all of his friends are in a similar situation and do the same thing on a regular basis?"

"While I don't know his friends and I can't say this with total certainty. I really doubt any of them are doing this with their sons," Margaret says in a tone that is both sympathetic and firm. "This type of sociopathic behavior is extremely abnormal and his telling you, 'everyone is doing it,' is something called Normalizing, it is a very common trait of someone with NPD."

"Normalizing?" I ask.

"Normalizing is a tactic used by narcissists to desensitize an individual to abuse or to coerce them into accepting the abnormal behavior as normal," Margaret tells me patiently. "When he told you that 'all of his friends' were doing it, you took him at his word, and that removed the social stigma from what he was asking you to help him with."

"What if a small group of his friends really is doing this type of stuff?" I ask her, as I continue to try and rationalize his actions.

"That doesn't make it any more right, and you know it," she says sympathetically. "I know it is difficult for you to accept that your father doesn't have your best interests at heart, but you need to start thinking of your own safety and well-being."

"My safety?" I ask, and then I continue to defend my father's actions. "I know this is really weird but other than Vegas, I haven't been in any situations that come close to life threatening."

"Your physical life doesn't have to be put in direct jeopardy for you to be put in harm's way." Margaret counters calmly. "In the year and a half since you have been involved with "Johnny," you have bought two motorcycles, relapsed into drinking again, isolated yourself from your loved ones and are taking unnecessary risks with your personal safety."

"Cancun was just-"

"David, I am not criticizing you. I am simply trying to get you to see the affect your father's behavior is having on your well-being. Ten minutes ago, you told me about your weekend joyrides on your motorcycles," she tells me in a matter of fact tone that reminds me of the tone I use when I am explaining the obvious to clients. "If you don't talk about them, your emotions just come out in other areas of your life. Just think about it."

Luckily, at that moment, the timer buzzes indicating my time is up for this session.

I walked out of my first session with Margaret more than a little dazed. I tried to sift through all of the information she had just given me as I walked to my car. While her diagnosis-from-afar felt right and gave me some relief, I couldn't let it go, not even to protect myself. I wanted to learn more about what might be wrong with my father.

As soon as I got home, I Googled the traits and symptoms of someone afflicted with Narcissistic Personality Disorder:

Lack of Empathy (Check)

Exploitive of Others (Check)

Envious of Others (Check)

Strong Sense of Entitlement (Check)

Only Thinks of Self (Check)

Grandiose Sense of Self Importance (Check)

My father could have been the poster boy for every single symptom. There wasn't even a "maybe" among them.

In addition to going to Margaret to deal with the emotional fallout, I started to go back to the rooms of AA. I didn't want to drink anymore. I wanted to build a life for myself that wasn't based on lies and manipulation. I knew I was broken, but for the first time in my life, I wanted to heal.

I wanted to be a better man.

This time in AA, I decided to pay attention to all the things they said in the rooms. I would refrain from forming opinions about it but simply *do the work*. I was willing to do whatever it took.

One of the biggest factors in staying sober is going to meetings on a consistent basis.

Before my first trip to Montreal with my father, I hadn't been to a meeting in a year. I had stopped going to meetings because I felt I didn't need them. After all, I had stopped drinking. The thing I finally realized is that going to meetings is like working out: the more you do it, the better shape you are in when things get bad.

During my first stint attending AA meetings, I sat at the back of the room and made sure I was the first guy out the door. This time, I went to the meetings after the meeting. The "meetings after the meeting" is a less formal group conversation after the meeting is over. That's usually where some very sage advice is dispensed.

I also made some friends in the rooms. It turned out some of the other AA members rode motorcycles as well. I met a guy named Mike at one of my meetings. While I normally rode alone, Mike had invited me to ride with him, and we started hitting the canyons of Malibu. I was finally connecting with good people.

I tried the best I could to follow all of the rules and practices of the AA program. I sure as hell didn't want to have to do it a third time. The truth is that if I relapsed again, I wasn't sure I would ever come back. I had allowed my life to become so dark, that I started to believe that there was no hope for me. Like Alison, I had almost allowed the darkness to take away my hope for a better life.

In my sessions with Margaret, I let everything out. The more I described the cruelty my father practiced, the more horrified she became at his behavior. She had seen the family dynamic first-hand years before, but even she was shocked at how bad things had gotten.

Part of the reason I had been so confused by my father's actions is that not everything my father did was wrong. I did learn some valuable lessons from him growing up. When I was a kid, Margaret had helped me to see some of the positive aspects of my childhood.

For example, he helped me get my first job.

I was 13 and working for our gardener at the height of Texas summer heat wave. The average temperature was about 105 degrees, and a number of people died from heatstroke when the temperatures went up further. My father felt my mother had weakened me by pampering me as a kid, and he was determined to "toughen me up." Our gardener would pick me up at 7 am in the morning and drop me off at 6:30 or 7 pm every night.

I got into the best shape of my life that summer. While the work was backbreaking and there were times I wanted to collapse, it taught me a very important rule: *never give up*. I realized I was far more capable than I thought and you can accomplish anything if you set your mind to it.

But it was occasionally dangerous work, and I was totally unsupervised.

Once I was pruning a tree with a chainsaw at about 7 pm when I almost cut off my leg. It was really dark, and I had misjudged the size of the branch and cut through it too quickly. The chainsaw leapt at my left leg, which was holding me up in the tree, and I thought, *I'M GOING TO CUT OFF MY LEG!* A small branch as thick as a pen stopped the chainsaw about an inch from my leg.

I learned another important lesson that day: to expect the unexpected because you can lose everything in an instant.

I also learned self-reliance from my father, because I knew I couldn't depend on anything he said. He would agree to help me with something (big or small) only to pull out at the last moment to see how I would handle it. Instead of feeling sorry for myself, I always tried to look for the lessons in the things my father did to me. Somehow, I always managed to find a way to convince myself of how he was "really" looking out for me.

I even gave my father and Maria credit for their constant rejections, as it allowed me to develop a very thick skin. That thick skin prepared me for the rejection my business throws at me on a daily basis. The truth is, I've made a pretty good living turning a "no" into a "yes" where it is appropriate. Countless times, on the phone with buyers telling me they didn't want to hire my client or buy a project, I would listen to their reasons instead of arguing. When appropriate, when I sensed there was a chance to turn it around, I would build my case. I never let their initial rejection deter me from my ultimate goal; after all, I was raised with rejection.

All my life, I was always trying to turn that "no" into a "yes."

However, it all backfired when I applied it to this situation. I had been raised my whole life to accept being treated as "less than worthy" of affection, attention, respect or compassion from my family. Now that I had gotten back into therapy, Margaret began to pull apart my father's most recent behavior, pointing out the pattern and tactics he used against me.

"Your father has put you in a 'no win' situation, David," Margaret tells me in a clinical but compassionate voice. "After you were isolated from the family, he used his position as your father to get what he wanted."

"Margaret, no one put a gun to my head," I tell her as I continue to defend my father. "I am a man, and I knew the risks."

"Should you have known better?" Margaret replies in a matter of fact voice. "Yes. In a perfect world, you should have walked away. However, he put you in the position of not only abandoning him but your grandmother and sisters as well. He used your desires to be a part of his family, to protect your grandmother and sisters, against you. Essentially he gave you two bad choices and made you choose."

"I have to take responsibility for my actions Margaret," I shoot back. "I am not a child."

Margaret just looked at me for a moment. I believe she knew I wasn't ready to hear *everything* at that moment, and there was only so much I was willing to accept. I think she knew I needed more time.

Years later, I would see the pattern for what it was and realize Margaret was 100% right on the money with her diagnosis. Sadly, when my father had finally decided to spend time with me, I was willing to accept that "quality time" in any form he deemed fit. I would have immediately rejected this type of "quality time" in any other form, but under the guise of "bonding with my father," I was blinded to the obvious.

In our next session, I tell her my biggest fear.

"I am really worried I am going to end up turning out just like him," I say. "There has to be some reason he shared this with me, something he saw in me, right?"

"David, you are *nothing* like him. It's obviously tearing you apart," she tells me sincerely as she shakes her head. "Being here *proves* you are nothing like him. The only thing he saw in you was your desire to be loved and accepted as a son. That presented an opportunity to get him what he wanted, nothing more."

"But I am his son, and that means it is possible for me to turn out like him," I argue. "I share this guys DNA!"

"Everyone has the power to determine who they are and who they want to be for themselves," Margaret says patiently. "It's called self-determination and your being here proves that point. You have made the decision that you want to be a better man than your father by rejecting what he was doing. DNA has nothing to do with it."

"Then why would he risk exposing me to all of this?" I ask. "Having a son is really important to my father. It's the only reason he has kept me around all of these years."

"To a narcissist, having a 'son' or 'daughter' has nothing to do with loving them or having any type of meaningful relationship. Children are simple possessions that have a sole purpose of enhancing their life," she says sadly, but I think she sees the confusion on my face as she continues to try and explain. "David, narcissists don't see other people like you, and I do. They only see themselves and what benefits them. To your father, you exist only to make him look good. You are like an accessory to him, something that enhances his image."

"You're saying I am like a pair of sunglasses to my father?" I croak back as a big lump has developed in my throat, and then I go into damage control mode. "Is there anything I can do to help him?"

"I know this hurts, David, but I want you to know what you are dealing with. You need to start protecting yourself emotionally, or you will continue to get hurt," she tells me with compassion in her eyes. "People suffering from NPD don't want to 'get well,' because they don't believe anything is wrong with them. They are only concerned with their own self-interest and have no empathy for others. They will take everything they can from you without giving the consequences a second thought."

Luckily, the buzzer went off indicating our time was up for this session. At that moment, I didn't think I could take much more.

As I walked to my car after that session, everything Margaret told me started to hit home. But as logical as everything sounded, I was still fighting decades of my father's programming and unwilling to accept what she was telling me. As I started my car, I decided there was only one way to really know if she was right, I had to test my father.

I came up with a way to certify in no uncertain terms, that my father really was "Johnny Russell – The Textbook Narcissist." I had to be certain that my father had no interest in or affection for me as a son. This test would not only give me an answer, but it would also get me off the hook for any future trips.

In the spirit of honesty, one of the tenets of AA, I told my father that I had relapsed because of the trips.

He knew I was an alcoholic.

In my early thirties, I was drinking so excessively that I called my mom one night and told her I needed to go to the Rehab. I didn't know what else to do, and I had hidden it from everyone. I later found out that my grandfather was an alcoholic; he died of cirrhosis of the liver. Given that alcoholism is genetic, this would have been nice to know before I started drinking ... but ours is a family of secrets.

I decided to tell my father that the brothels, prostitutes and lies were a trigger for my drinking. I would tell him that I simply couldn't do the trips and stay sober anymore. How he handled my obvious need to end my involvement in the trips would tell me how he really felt about me. I was hoping he would shelve the trips, put away his double life, and agree to go fishing with me, or hunting, or to a game.

Anything.

I let the whole family know I relapsed as well; honesty is a big part of the program. I just didn't tell them why. That way, I was mostly honest, contained the fallout and protected my family from the truth.

To his credit, my father initially expressed concern over the relapse and told me I didn't have to go on any more of those trips with him. I made it clear that I was happy to do normal father-son things with him, like fishing and hunting, but I had to draw the lines at whorehouses.

But he wasn't interested in hunting or fishing. Or in me. Once the whorehouses were off the table, he went from calling me once a week to not calling me at all. He waited three weeks to "check in" on me after I told him I couldn't be his brother/beard/cleaner anymore. Margaret had warned me that he was isolating me, as a way to punish me for no longer enabling his behavior.

I didn't want to believe my father was using this type of manipulation tactic on me. It was bad enough to see him play games with the prostitutes, but I refused to believe he would do this with his own son. Our conversation that day was one I will never forget...

"Hey, David, I am just calling to check in and see how you are doing," he says, and I notice he didn't start this conversation with "son" the way he normal does.

"I am doing fine. I am going to ninety meetings in ninety days like they tell you to do in the program," I reply, and the truth is I feel better than I have in years. "How are the girls doing?"

"They are doing fine, and I am proud that you have fixed your problem," he says, but I immediately pick up on the critical tone. "I don't think any less of you, now that you have put your problems behind you. You know I have always been there for you when you have had your problems in the past with alcohol."

"I know," I say, even though the only involvement my father has ever had with my recovery was bringing my grandmother to visit me in rehab. I always suspected he did that to weaken me in her eyes, and it feels like he is setting me up for something new now.

"I'm sorry, Dad. It just got to be too much for me," I say trying to close the subject.

"Do you know what it was about the trips that made you start drinking again?" he asks and when I don't respond he continues. "What I am saying is that, since you have put this behind you, is there anything I could modify so we could still do the trips?"

"I am not sure that would work, Dad." I manage to say as I am almost speechless. "The trip-"

"What if I got the girls their own room?" he interjects. "That way you would know that you wouldn't have to share a room with them. That's what started all the trouble, was when you had to share your room in Vegas. Would you at least be willing to try it out?"

A wave of emotions starts to overwhelm me, but I immediately start to suppress them. At that moment, I want to scream out in anger, but I can't find the words.

How can you even ask me to keep doing this you selfish bastard!!! I think to myself. *I told you specifically that it was the prostitutes, the lying and the abusive behavior that made me relapse. Don't you care about me at all?*

Of course, I don't say what I am thinking. As usual, I compartmentalize my feelings and bottle them up. I tell him only part of the truth. "I don't think that would work Dad. It isn't really the sleeping arrangements that are the trigger for me as much as what happens on the trips. It just feels like I'm a third wheel and you are consumed with whoever you are with," I say calmly and then add, "I also don't like how things end."

I couldn't believe my father was willing to risk my basic health so that he could spend nine hours a day in a brothel in some foreign city. As much as I didn't want to admit it, there was no way to deny Margaret had been right about everything.

"Well obviously, I don't want you doing something you aren't strong enough to handle," he replies with a very disappointed tone but then brightens. "But it was so much fun being able to share this with you and spend time together! The girls were just a bonus."

He spent 85% of those trips with the "bonus," and only ate his meals with me.

He quickly ends the call, when it becomes obvious to him that his brother/beard/cleaner has retired. He stopped calling me after that; like my sisters, he simply lost my number. I still talked with my grandmother, but I knew I would be "officially" and fully rejected from the family when she left this earth.

I know it is wrong, but I wish my father had just hit me.

There would have been honesty in the physical abuse, and I would have been able to defend myself eventually. I am not saying a father should hit his son, but in this situation it would have been much more direct and honest reflection of what my father thought of me.

After all of this, I still believe family is the most important part of your life, the thing you put above all else. You just have to make sure they actually *love you*.

I continued to see Margaret when I could, as our sessions offered the first bit of relief I'd felt since the whole process began. Releasing those emotions was as powerful as blowing off the steam built up inside a pressure cooker; the shame, regret, anger, disbelief, shock, betrayal, rejection and pain I had been carrying with me created a weight that was crushing my soul.

I thought of those emotions like they were bricks in a backpack that I could never take off.

Whenever you carry a secret like this or behave in a way that degrades you as a person, the emotional equivalent of a brick is added to the backpack. This backpack was something I lived with every waking moment, but I rarely looked inside to see what I was carrying. I just kept trudging along under its weight, and it affected everything I did.

Over time, as the backpacks weight increased, it started to prevent me from being open with other people and forming bonds that are critical to a sense of contentment. It robbed me of the ability to be truly happy by trusting others and sharing my life with them. In short, it blocked me from making healthy choices.

I knew how heavy my backpack was, and I even had an idea of what carrying it was costing me. But I was so ashamed that until I started seeing Margaret, I didn't have the courage to look inside it and take inventory.

Going to Margaret was the first critical step of healing.

Finding the courage to look inside the backpack was empowering. Taking apart, identifying and talking about each brick allows you to lighten the load until one day, you're able put the backpack down. Going through that process is painful, messy and really hard, but it's the only way to gain your strength back, and become healthy again.

One of the things I have learned in all of this is to spend as much time as you can with those people who do treat you with love and affection. Push the negativity and darkness out of your life and keep the people who are positive and happy as close to you as possible. They are the light that allows you to see the good in the world.

It was around this time Veronica bought a house 30 minutes away from where I lived.

Veronica is my sister. We aren't related by blood, but she's still my sister in every other sense of the word. My mother remarried when I was 11, and Veronica is her husband's daughter from his first marriage. We grew up together, and she is truly one of the best things that has ever happened to me.

She was married to a great guy named Kyle, and they had kids of their own. On the way to their new house was a stretch of winding road called Latigo Canyon in Malibu. It was my favorite place to ride my motorcycle, as it demanded total focus and concentration; many riders had gone off its cliffs.

There was no room for both Latigo Canyon and "Johnny Russell" in my head. The faster I rode, the freer of him I felt.

I found myself riding to Veronica's house every weekend. Ever the proud uncle, I have tried to be at every major event in her children's lives from their birth to birthdays. Kyle is a terrific father, and their children have been raised in an atmosphere of love, encouragement, and happiness. You literally can see how loved they are in their eyes. It felt good just being around them and experiencing that type of family dynamic.

They had become the only bright spots in the dark life I had been leading.

There is also such a freedom and exhilaration riding motorcycles. You connect to the road and the bike in a way that they almost become a part of you. I also enjoyed the camaraderie with other riders; it gave me a sense of belonging and connection, something I really wanted.

I spent every penny I had on my motorcycles and safety gear, sparing no expense. I had a Yamaha R1 (basically a race bike with lights) and a Laverda 750 (one of only two or three in California) along with $3500 worth of safety equipment.

I knew riding was dangerous, but it gave me a freedom I hadn't felt in a long time. I loved it. Before I bought the motorcycles, I took out a $500,000.00 life insurance policy in case something happened to me. I made Veronica and her children my beneficiaries. I wanted to make sure that the people who treated me with love and affection were taken care of in case something happened to me.

Part of the reason I love motorcycles was that when I was a boy, my grandfather bought me one, and we would ride it together. I enjoyed this happy association with a positive male role model in my life. I had two loving grandfathers when I was a child (yes, "Johnny's" father was a wonderful man), and in a weird way, my riding felt like I was connecting with my grandfather again.

I spent more and more time at my sister's house, often helping with home improvement work. That job gave me insight into the type of person I wished my father was – in the form of Veronica's stepfather, Pete.

Pete impressed me immensely. He loved my sister the way a father should love a child, even after she's grown. Pete was a one man building crew, and he was on a mission. An architect by trade, he would literally pack all of his construction gear in bags and fly to L.A. to work on Veronica's house. He had 25 or 30 years on me but worked me into the ground.

He was the type of guy who rarely spoke but got the job done right the first time. His love for my sister was quiet and solid; he built her and her husband a walk in closet and a window in her bedroom. We were working on the deck above my sister's carport when we started talking.

"Hey Pete, when was the last time you took a vacation?" I ask him as we are hauling up 2x4's to the top of the carport to start framing the deck.

"I am on vacation now, David," Pete answers with a smile.

"No, a real vacation, when you are not taking care of Veronica or building something," I say laughing at the thought of working a 12 hour day doing construction being his idea of a vacation.

Pete smiles down at me as he lifts up the next 2x4 I have handed him and he says, "This is my vacation, I get to see my grandkids, I get to take care of my daughter, and most importantly I get a chance to show them how much they mean to me. I am lucky I get to do this with my time off."

It was the most Pete and I talked while we were working, but those few words gave me a great insight into what a good father looks like. Pete's actions – the way he spent his time and his experience and his sweat – showed over and over how much he loved my sister. He acted like a father, and he was a stark contrast to my own father.

I couldn't even imagine the words, "You want to split her?" coming out of Pete's mouth.

Pete valued his daughter, and his actions showed how he felt. Words to someone like Pete had very little meaning unless they were backed up with action. I am sure in his mind, they were just a waste of time.

The truth is that I was looking at everything differently at this point. I had started to reassess my life based on actions and not words. While my father's transparent actions had gutted me emotionally, I was still trying to find the light in my life.

As much as Margaret was helping me at that time, I wasn't completely willing to accept my father's actions for what they were. Because of that, I didn't address the emotions that stemmed from those actions and Margaret was right; they came out in other areas of my life.

One of those areas was the way I rode my motorcycle.

I admit now that there were times when I rode that I pressed too hard and went too fast. I didn't fully understand the gift of life that God had given me. I was trying to escape the demons I refused to confront. On my bike, I would often lapse back into the negative thinking I was raised with and because of it, I didn't always value myself or consider my life the precious gift it is.

I know now that God was watching out for me during the time I was riding. I took a lot of risks, but somehow always managed to get home safely. It's hard for me to look back on that time without thinking, *You were a total idiot!* But I was a lucky idiot.

And my luck was about to run out.

CHAPTER SEVEN

WHEN YOUR LUCK RUNS OUT...

A lot of good things were happening in my life. I had six weeks of continuous sobriety. I was finding positive people to spend my time with. I had just gotten a green light on a low-budget feature film I was producing, and I represented the producer on *Sin City 2*, which was finally getting made in my home state of Texas.

It had taken a lot of blood and sweat to achieve all this, and there were a lot of times when I didn't think I was going to make it. But I had managed to keep my company afloat through the crisis of 2008, and I was finally starting to see all my hard work pay off.

The only dark spot in my life was my father and how he had used me.

I had always believed that my father's absence from my life was because Maria hated me with such a passion. She took every shot she could at me and he never tried to stop it. I always assumed he was just trying to keep the peace for my sisters' sake, but after sitting down with Margaret,

I began to question if that was his real reason.

I had never thought of it before, but the last blowout I had with Maria, the girls were in their mid 20s and lived in their own houses. His fallback of "I am doing it for the girls," didn't really track, but at that point, I had become used to the abuse. Taking the hits from Maria was just the cost of getting to see my family.

That trip had started out like all of the others. Maria started in on me the second I got there, but I did my best to avoid her. I had flown out to spend time with my family, but my main goal was to spend as much time as I could with my grandmother. Unfortunately, I had forgotten to print out some scripts for work and asked Maria if I could print them out on her printer.

I should have known better...

"How many pages do you want to print out?" she asks me in a tone that tells me she is looking for a fight.

"I am not sure, but it couldn't be more than 200 pages." I answer quickly and try to diffuse the situation by taking a 20 dollar bill out of my wallet and handing it to her as I say sincerely, "I am happy to pay for whatever ink and paper I use. I wouldn't ask, but I have to read the script before work on Monday. I would really appreciate it if you could help me out with this."

Maria looks down at the 20 dollar bill in my hand. Her eyes narrow as she takes it.

"I don't know," she says in a taunting tone. "That's a lot of ink and paper. Let me ask my assistant if this will be enough to cover it."

My stepmother took the 20 dollars to her home office ... located in another wing of the house. Maria and my father have spent around a half a million dollars on each of my sisters Ivy League educations. This doesn't take into account their homes, cars, trips, and all of the other things I am thankful they have. I have asked my father and Maria for almost nothing my entire life, and whenever I do, they rub my nose in it, like this.

Worse, they act as if their wealth has nothing to do with my grandmother's good fortune and generosity. I had even bent over backward to get my grandmother to forgive Maria for the mistreatment I suffered at her hands when I was a kid. Now she is giving me a hard time over printing out a couple of scripts?

Had she just taken the money, I would have been fine with it, but she had to stick the knife in a little deeper.

I was done.

I don't say anything; I just take a 6-mile hike to cool my head. If this had been a one-time thing, I would have let it slide, but this type of stuff constantly happened with Maria. She never missed an opportunity take a shot at me because she knew there would never be any fallout with my father. For my entire life, he has turned a blind eye to it.

After 30 years of being treated like an unwanted bastard stepchild, I had finally had enough.

During the walk, I decide I won't get into it with Maria, but simply grant her wish and leave the house. I call Veronica and tell her what just happened. I want to be sure I am not overreacting.

"Come home," she says immediately after I finish filling her in. "You don't deserve this."

When I get back to the house, the maid lets me in. For my entire life, I have never been allowed to have a key or to know the house's security code – another not so subtle reminder that I am an unwanted guest. I decide to keep things as civil as possible with Maria, regarding my departure.

In what I hope will be my last conversation with her, I stand at the front door with my bags in hand and I am as honest as I can be.

"Listen, I get it, you hate me, and that's OK. Sometimes people just don't get along. I get it now, and I will no longer come here and bother you anymore. I just want to thank you for taking such good care of my sisters and my Grandma."

She could have smiled, nodded and said: "You're welcome and goodbye."

Instead, her eyes narrowed again as she taps into my biggest fear. "Well, maybe I won't take care of your grandmother anymore," she shoots back with menace in her voice.

"No, no. That's OK. No need to go there, I am gone," I promise as I hurry out the door with my bags.

Maria did well that day. She made twenty bucks, finally got rid of the stepchild she couldn't stand ... and she didn't even print out the scripts.

My love for my grandmother was my Achilles heel, and Maria knew it.

As a former pharmacist, she was responsible for the medications my father prescribed for my grandmother and monitored when they were refilled. That and the fact she was responsible for all of the other details of my grandmother's life, from how fast her air-conditioning got fixed in the summer to the safety equipment in her bathroom shower made me back down every time.

Before my blow up with Maria on that same trip, my grandmother broke down again in tears of regret and guilt, thinking about my childhood. "I tried to protect you the best way I knew how. That's why I always took you to the Ranch with me when you were young; I figured you would be safe there."

"Don't worry about it, Grandma, you did a great job," I told her as I always minimized what happened in the past. "I'm fine, and I forgave Maria a long time ago. I just want you to enjoy your life now."

While I never shared the new stuff with my grandmother, I did my best to minimize the past. The simple fact was I was scared she would try to make things right, and I knew Maria would crush her for it. It wouldn't take too much for Maria to take away the most precious thing in my life.

In hindsight, I realize that instead of just denying how my father and Maria's abusive behavior affected me, I should have taken out the bricks my grandmother was pointing to in my backpack and talked with her about them. Like Margaret, she wanted to help me, by getting me to acknowledge what was happening, instead of continuing to suppress my feelings and live in denial.

My grandmother knew my denial ran deep and ignoring it was only making things worse for me.

When I finally started looking at the bricks that I was carrying in my backpack with Margaret, I started to open my eyes to why my grandmother was so worried about how I had been treated growing up. I began to see that my father's ambivalence toward protecting me from Maria had nothing to do with my not being worthy of protection, but simply revealed he only cared about himself.

Both my grandmother and Margaret were trying to point out the profound effect all of this had on me, but still I wasn't strong enough to see things for what they were, instead of what I wanted them to be.

"The effects of being treated this way by your family not only manifest themselves in negative behavior like your drinking, David," Margaret would tell me. "You have to be careful that you don't accept the values that they have given you as your own."

I heard her words, but I refused to see the truth in what she was saying. Instead of acknowledging the pain, I continued to cover it up by acting as if it didn't affect me.

I am a man, I thought. *I am immune to feeling the pain of their rejection at this point in my life.*

"Don't worry about it. Margaret. I know I'm not the piece of garbage they think I am!" I joked as I tried to get off the subject. "I know I am not a bad guy."

Looking back on it now, I realize both Margaret and my grandmother were trying to point out the obvious to me: I had accepted the value my family had placed on me, as my own. I had been treated as a second class citizen by my family for so long that deep down, I really held the same low opinion of myself that they did.

Somewhere in my mind, I had learned to value myself as "less than."

Once I met Johnny Russell, things grew worse quickly. I had been raised with the core belief that life only has value after it hits some type of marker or level of success. Those markers had been established by my family in the forms of scholastic achievement, social position, and financial success. Since I didn't attend an Ivy League school or have a million dollars in the bank, I knew in their minds I didn't measure up.

When my father failed the test I gave him, it confirmed my worst fear. In his mind I really was expendable, and it destroyed any sense of value I had left in myself at the time. As ashamed as I am to admit it, even after everything, I had still wanted my father to love and value me. When I realized this wasn't going to happen, I started to act out, and I started to take risks I knew I shouldn't take.

I would like to say the water park in Mexico was the beginning of that risk-taking behavior, but it really began when I bought the motorcycles. I didn't realize then, but now I know I started to value my life the same way my father and his family had.

I stopped valuing the most precious gift God had given me, *my life*.

I don't remember a lot from that day, thankfully. I was riding with my friend Mike from AA and I only remember coming to after it happened. At that moment, I realized that this time I wasn't going to be able to get up and keep going.

Until I started writing this, I asked Mike not to tell me about the accident itself. I wanted to put this one in my rearview mirror. I wasn't ready to look at that brick in my backpack.

Mulholland Drive – Los Angeles, California: July 1st, 2012.

We were riding on the legendary Mulholland Drive in the Malibu canyons, and a group of bikes flew past us. I guess I decided to catch up with them.

"When I saw the bikes fly past us, my first thought was 'please don't!' But you took off," Mike said. "You kept up with them until you went into the second right-hander. Something spooked you, and you hesitated. You hit your brakes instead of pushing through and pulled out of the turn."

I have seen other people do this, and I know what happens from there. It's a rookie maneuver, and I don't know why I did it. I don't know if I will ever remember what was going through my mind at that moment, but this accident changed my life forever.

"You went over your bike," he continued. "You and your bike slid towards the cliff at about 25 miles an hour." His voice gets choked up at the memory. "That's when you hit the only telephone pole within half a mile. Your body literally bounced off it."

Mike no longer rides.

"I finally caught up to where you went down." He pauses for a second to calm himself. "When I got to you, you weren't breathing. I raised the visor on your helmet and tried to feel for a pulse." He pauses again. "Then you kind of croaked like you'd swallowed your tongue or something and you tried to breathe. I thought you were dead. Two guys on pedal bikes rode up and told me to get out of the way. They were Orthopedic Surgeons and saw you take the hit. They started to stabilize you."

This is where my memory picks up, and I remember opening my eyes and seeing a guy in cycling gear standing over me.

"I am a physician, and I want to help you. Do I have your permission to examine you?" one of the Doctors in cycling gear asks me.

"Yes, I won't sue and thanks for helping me," I reply quickly. I was finding it difficult to breathe. I knew a lot of doctors were leery of offering roadside assistance for fear of lawsuits.

"I'm amazed you're alive!" he says as he unzips my leathers. "My friend and I saw you go down, and we started sprinting over here on our bikes." He sees my chest and back protector and says, "This saved your life."

He lifts my chest protector and puts his ear to my chest to listen in several places.

The pain is starting to hit now that the shock is wearing off, and *I hurt everywhere*. The pain is excruciating.

Obviously unhappy with the sound of my breathing, the surgeon gives his friend a look. "Do I have your permission to perform an emergency tracheotomy on you, if your breathing gets worse?"

SHIT!

This is what I feared he would say, but I reply calmly, "Yes, but I would rather do that in a hospital." He nods and asks his friend to come over and help. "Does anyone have a pocket knife I can use?"

NO, NO, NO, NO!!!! PLEASE let this be a dream! I think desperately as someone hands him a pocket knife.

I had pressed my luck too far, too often and now I was paying the price. The surgeon crew goes to work stabilizing me. Other than God, an amazing EMT crew, Life Flight, amazing surgeous, nurses, technicians and the hospital itself, I credit these surgeons for saving my life.

I didn't get your names, but if you are reading this, THANK YOU!

The pain is getting worse, steadily going from excruciating to feeling like I am on fire. When I try to move, the pain is so intense that I can't focus my eyes. I decide not to try to move again. EVER!

The surgeon opens a pocket knife and starts to inspect the blade. Sunlight glints off it, and I'm starting to realize that I am not dreaming this, it is really happening!

"Does anyone have something I can clean the blade off with?" the surgeon asks. "Water will work if we don't have anything else. Also, I need some type of tube to open the airway."

Someone hands him a water bottle and he starts to wash off the blade as he does his best to sterilize it. Someone else gives him a Bic pen, and he takes the ink out of it quickly. He looks at his friend and motions him to step behind my body.

"I am going to have my friend hold you still, so you don't move when I'm making the incision," he says calmly. "You need to stay as still as possible so that I can make a clean incision. This is going to hurt, but try not to move."

His friend grabs on to my shoulders and presses down to keep me still. *SHIT!!*

This is when I hear sirens wailing in the distance. I have never been so happy to hear that sound before in my life. The surgeon motions to his friend to let go of my shoulders.

Once the EMT guys arrive, they put me on oxygen immediately, as the doctor gives him a rundown of what is wrong with me. As soon as the oxygen hits, I get some strength back and start to move.

"Hey guys, maybe this isn't so bad," I say as I try to sit up, but they stop me. "I feel better now; I think I'm OK! Maybe I can get up."

They looked at each other, and I realize I am in real trouble.

"That's the oxygen," the EMT says quickly. "We're going to meet a Life Flight helicopter in five minutes in a field down the street. You need to get to a hospital immediately!"

Yep, I'm screwed, I think to myself.

One of the few benefits to being the son of a doctor is the knowledge that when you are put on a "Life Flight" helicopter, you're in real danger of dying. This is a drastic measure they are taking to save your life. Otherwise, an ambulance takes you to the hospital.

They quickly load me into the ambulance and race to an empty field about five minutes away. As I start thinking about what happens next, people continue to confirm my worst fears about the condition I am in.

Everyone keeps saying the same thing, "You're going to be all right, but we need to get you to the hospital *immediately!*" After hearing that for the third time from the EMT in the helicopter as they are strapping me in, I realize they are not just being cautious. Breathing is getting more difficult as we take off, and the oxygen isn't helping me as much. The pain is literally radiating through my body.

Am I even going to make it to the hospital? I start to wonder.

It's getting cold in the helicopter as we fly to the hospital. While I try to withstand the pain, I keep tripping up on my greatest regret: walking down that dark and painful path with my father. A year later, when I tell my father about the depth of my regret, he makes no comment. He simply doesn't acknowledge it.

However at that moment, I still wanted to believe that my father loved me, and I had done the right thing by protecting him and the family. This is when a thought flashes through my mind.

Will my father even care if I die? I wonder for the first time in my life.

Immediately, I feel guilty for even questioning my father's love. I realize now that not only was I raised to think I was expendable, but also to feel shame if I ever questioned my family's love. However, at that moment in the helicopter, with a very high possibility of dying from my injuries, I finally started to open my eyes and begin to examine "Johnny Russell's" real agenda.

As the helicopter starts to land, I even wondered if he won't actually feel a little relief if I die. The shock of the motorcycle accident and the possibility of death have loosened the shackles of my conditioning, and I start to do some critical thinking. I began to play things out in my head factoring in *what* I had seen "Johnny Russell" do on those five trips and how he behaved toward those women.

I was no longer going to be his brother/beard/cleaner and I no longer serve any real purpose to him. I think as I started to understand what Margaret was saying for the first time. I apply it to the situation I now face and realize. *My death will ensure that his secret life stays secret.*

I force this thought from my head. My conditioning takes hold again and I feel guilty for even suspecting my father would take joy in my passing. As they transfer me from the helicopter gurney to a waiting stretcher, my thoughts turned to my part in things.

I have tried to do the right thing for others, not myself, I think to myself desperately, as I hope it will count for something. *There was no personal gain in my covering for him, only protecting my grandmother and sisters from the truth.*

I start to prepare myself in case I die, by going through a brief checklist in my mind. My will covers all my working deals, which go into my estate to be distributed fairly. My life insurance is in place, so the people who treated me with love and kindness are taken care of. Everything is taken care of with the exception of two things.

I didn't make amends for my part in my father's double life, I think to myself regretfully, as they wheel me into the hospital. *And I never let myself trust someone enough to fall in love.*

Once I get into Pre-Op, things get very real, very quickly. I am immediately greeted by Dr. Wolf, the Chief of Trauma Surgery at the hospital. Apparently, when the helicopter radioed in my vitals, she was paged immediately. Growing up in hospitals, I know this is also not a good sign.

Normally interns do the intake and initial examination of new patients, not the Chief of Trauma Surgery. Her being there to examine me means I need to go into surgery immediately. She does a quick, but thorough examination and gets right to the point.

"We need to operate as soon as possible," Dr. Wolf tells me with no preliminaries, "I believe your spleen has ruptured, you have multiple perforations in your bowel, and both of your lungs are filling up with blood."

"OK, you have my permission to do whatever you need to do," I say without hesitation. I know I am in bad shape at this point but have to ask. "How bad is it?"

"First, we need to drain the blood filling up in your left lung right now. I am amazed you are still able to breathe normally," she says flatly. "As long as the lung doesn't collapse when we try to drain it, we will take you immediately to X-ray and for a CT scan. This will confirm both the ruptured spleen and bowel perforations. Hopefully, there will not be any more complications, and we can go straight into surgery. Time is a critical factor at this point, and I need you to sign your consent forms immediately."

"No problem and thanks for taking care of me," I say as I take the forms from her and start signing. After I finish signing about 50 forms, I lie there for a moment as a nurse starts to prepare me for the procedure right there in Pre-Op.

I feel the excess Betadine solution run down my side, as I prepare myself for what comes next. A moment later, Dr. Wolf comes back and makes an inch long incision through my rib cage. She inserts a clear tube into my lung, and I feel the pressure on my left lung start to release a little. I turn my head to the left, and I see blood running through the tube in my chest into some type of plastic bag hanging off the side of the gurney.

Luckily my lung doesn't collapse. I have cleared the first hurdle.

My buddies had asked me whom to call, and by then, my best friend Steve arrives at the hospital 30 minutes later. I didn't want to bother my mother and her husband, who were on a trip to Vegas. I really didn't want them to know at all; they were less than thrilled when I got the bikes.

"Hey buddy, I talked to the doctor, and you are going to be fine!" Steve tells me as soon as he walks into Pre-Op. We have been friends for 25 years, and I know when he is lying before he does.

I am totally screwed. I think to myself. *And it isn't just the tube draining blood out of my lung that is freaking him out. He is literally as white as a sheet!*

This is really, really bad.

Steve has seen me cut up before. He was the guy holding a compress against my head when I washed up onto the beach when we were 16 on a surf trip. My surfboard had cracked my head open, and I half paddled/half floated back to shore. He took care of the first aid on the beach, so I know he has a strong stomach.

Whatever they told him wasn't good.

"Is there anything I can get for you?" Steve asks. "I think I should call your mom."

"No," I say quickly. My mom doesn't deserve to watch me die; if it goes that way. "They are on a trip to Vegas, and I don't want to bother them. If you are cool hanging out here while I am in surgery, I think I am covered."

"OK, buddy. Whatever you say, but I think your mom would want to know," Steve says and then he sees my face. "Don't worry, I won't call her, and I will be here the entire time."

"Thanks man, I appreciate it. Sorry if I took you away from anything," I say as I am truly thankful someone will be waiting with me in Pre-Op.

The dull pain is growing more intense right now, and I am starting to get tired at the same time.

An ER nurse walks in and asks if she can cut off my leathers and I say go for it. The thought of trying to get them off exhausts me at this point. I feel the cold surgical steel of the scissors graze my legs and arms as they cut me out off my leathers.

I will soon learn that pain also manifests itself in the form of exhaustion. I was given something for the pain, but I still feel it anytime I move. The nurse lets Steve know that he needs to leave the Pre-Op room now, as they are about to start moving me.

As soon as Steve leaves, every emotion I have ever suppressed in my life hits me like a tidal wave. I am too tired to fake it or compartmentalize anymore. I finally allow myself to feel the guilt, shame, regret and anger for being "Johnny's" accomplice. The person I was most angry with wasn't "Johnny;" I was angry at myself for enabling him to hurt those women.

I deserve this, I think to myself. *I deserve the pain and I deserve to die for what I have allowed to happen.*

Then I start to think about how many people are trying to save me, and I feel even worse. A wave of self-loathing hits me, as I lie there waiting in Pre-Op.

I don't really deserve their time. I think, guilty as everyone here has shown me nothing but kindness and compassion. *I am not a good man.*

I look over at the doctors as they confer with each other.

If these people saw the real me, the one who enabled "Johnny" to do such horrible things, they would wheel me out of the ER and park me next to the garbage bins. I think as the self-loathing I feel reaches a fever pitch. *I am a piece of garbage that needs to be thrown away. Just ask my father.*

Two nurses enter the room and start unlocking the brakes on my gurney. That snaps me out of this dark moment, and one of the nurses tells me we need to get moving. *Now!*

"We need to get to X-ray as quickly as possible; I want to warn you we will be moving a little more quickly than you are used to. Please tell us if you start to feel extreme pain, and we will slow down a little," she tells me in a calm tone that I am getting familiar with at this point.

I know everyone is trying really hard not to worry me, but the truth is that I am becoming less and less worried about my well-being as time passes. We race down the hallway, with the female nurse clearing a path verbally, while a large male nurse really puts his back into getting me to X-ray "as quickly as possible."

At this point, I am pretty sure I am not going to make it, based on the reactions we are getting from the different departments we visit. It starts with the X-ray department. As soon as the X-ray tech starts giving the nurse a hard time for cutting to the front of the line, she whispers something in his ear. The tech immediately walks to the person he was about to X-ray and asks her to give me her spot.

At first, she protests and then the tech whispers in her ear. She looks over at me and quickly hops off the gurney, as they all move me off my gurney and into position on the X-ray table. After that, we race from X-ray to a CT scan department, and the same thing happens.

Now I know I am in serious trouble.

The ceiling tiles are becoming a blur as I sail from one department to the next. My anxiety is now completely gone, and I am really getting sleepy. I start to drift off into unconsciousness, but I am then yanked back by the pain every time we take a turn too quickly or bump into something.

I am not only physically exhausted, but mentally exhausted too.

I have been carrying those bricks in my backpack for so long, that the thought of finally getting rid of them is a happy one, even if it means I have to die to be free of them. I know the drugs and pain are screwing with my thoughts, so I try to rally. I try to convince myself that I am still worthy of these people's care and that I need to fight.

Your actions and your words are all that you take with you in this life. I think to myself as I try to build my strength for whatever comes next. *Other than the thing with your father, you have lived a pretty good life.*

I had always treated people the way I wanted to be treated. I was kind to strangers as well as friends and helped people in need with no desire to be paid back. I was honest in all of my affairs, but one. While it didn't add up to a perfect life, it reflected that most of the core principles I practiced were solid ones.

They finally wheel me into the operating theater, and I am surrounded by bright lights and lots of machines, as they transfer me from the gurney to the operating table. For the first time since I woke up from the crash, I feel a sense of closure, whatever happens next is out of my hands, and I know it.

I came close to turning it around, I think to myself as they start to put me under. *I just didn't have enough time. I changed course and started to walk down the right path. Maybe that will count for something?*

I had no way of knowing that I was about to enter a coma for more than three weeks, that I would take a journey few people come back from, and that when I was brought back to this world, my eyes would be truly open for the first time in my life.

It is in God's hands now. That was my last thought before I lost consciousness...

On the ranch as a kid getting ready to lead horses into horse trailer

My first date at the Velma picnic when I was a kid

Feeding a calf my grandmother gave me as a kid

First prize I ever won as a kid

First trip to Montreal

My La Verde 750 and Yamada R1

View out of the plane before I flew to Montreal for second trip

Second Vegas trip

Working on the carport deck with Pete and my niece

Sunset in Cancun

Riding on Mulholland Drive on my La Verda 750

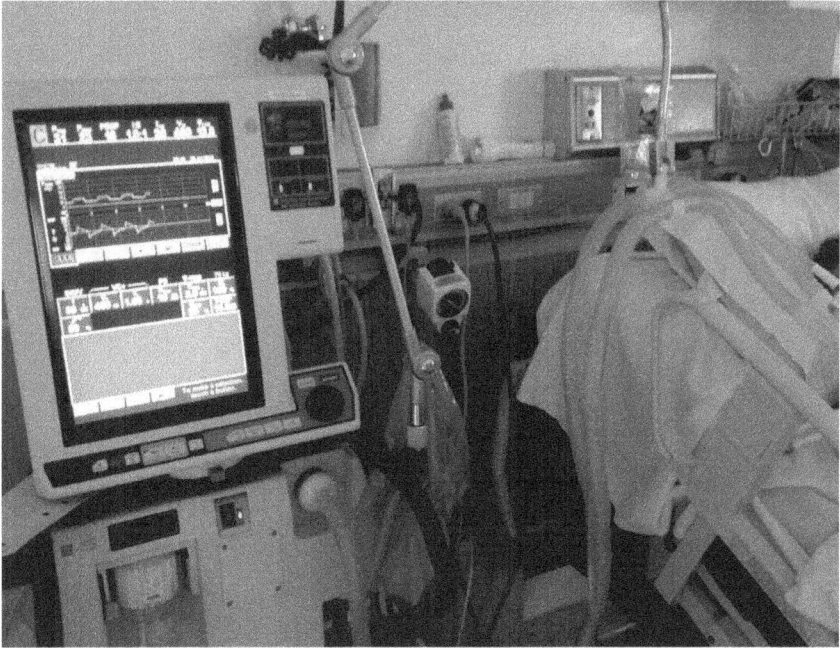

The ventilator that kept me alive

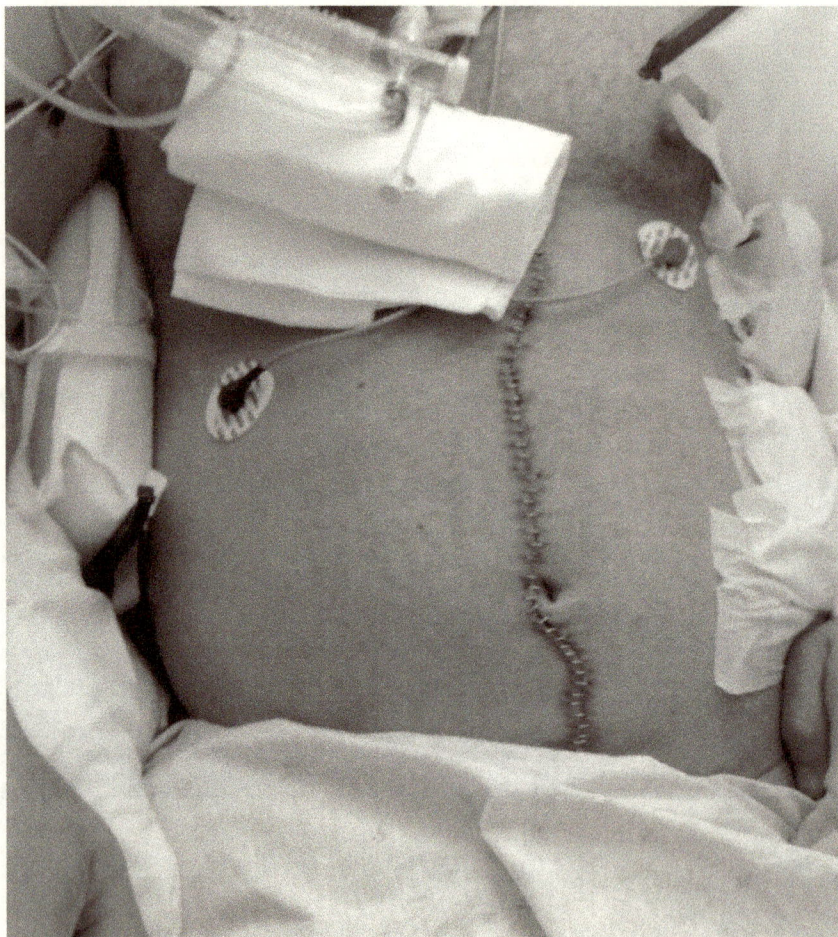

My body swelled up to 3 times its normal size

Me in my grandfathers chair, which I still have

First day of shooting on set of film I produced after accident

San Francisco trip

CHAPTER EIGHT

COMA AND RECOVERY

Faith is a funny thing.

Depending on where you put it, it can bring you great joy or sorrow. I believe it is God's greatest gift to us. Each action in our lives is an expression of faith or a lack of it. Faith is how one builds a life, one choice at a time.

I had taken part in my father's sordid double life because I had faith that underneath all of his depravity and selfishness, there was a good man, a man worth saving. Even deeper in my heart, I had faith in the most basic principle of all, that my father loved his son, the last male Davis. It would take this motorcycle accident and what I would see next to break that faith in my father and finally keep my eyes open.

Luckily, I also had faith in a power greater than myself. Before the anesthesia took hold of me, I put my faith in that higher power to see me through this. I knew God was looking out for me and what happened next would confirm this faith in a way that would change my life forever.

For a year and a half, I had ridden alone, often at night, charging through the canyons to escape the thoughts in my head. The first time I went down, I was immediately surrounded by people who only had one goal: to save me.

Two orthopedic surgeons just happened to be biking up the road I crashed on.

"From the moment you went down, things went off like clockwork," Mike said when he was telling me what happened the day of my accident. "The ambulance was there ten minutes after you bounced off the telephone pole and the helicopter was waiting for you once we got to the field. I have never seen a group of people more determined to save a person's life."

I believe God put those Orthopedic Surgeons on the road that day, the same way he put that small branch in front of the chainsaw and protected my leg when I was a kid. There was a reason I had lived this long, but I just hadn't seen it yet.

This accident was the first step toward a greater understanding of my purpose in life. I didn't realize it at the time, but I had an obligation to make amends for my part in things with "Johnny Russell." I was going to be given a choice whether I was to stay here and fulfill that obligation, or to let go and leave this world.

Until I started writing this, I asked my sister Veronica, Steve and my mother not to tell me what happened the day of the accident. I didn't see any point in reliving such a painful part of my life. However, I now realize that I should give credit to the people who heroically fought to save my life and the family members that stood by me in my time of need.

My mother arrived at the hospital after I had been in surgery for 4 hours. Dr. Wolf came out of the OR to give her a brief update. As usual, she said exactly what was on her mind the moment she saw her.

"They should have brought your son here in a box," Dr. Wolf said to my mother as soon as she walked into the waiting room. "I don't know how he's still alive!"

As soon as my mother heard this, her legs started to give out, and Dr. Wolf immediately moved to help her into a chair. When my mother tells me this story, I instantly picture Dr. Wolf, a thin 5-foot-4-inch Filipino women helping my mother, a voluptuous and 6-foot-tall blond women, into of one the tiny chairs in the waiting room next to the OR.

"I am sorry, but the nurse told me you were a doctor?" Dr. Wolf said in response to my mother's reaction. "I assumed that you would want me to be as candid as possible about his condition."

"I am a psychologist, but please be as candid as you can," my mother replied faintly.

"Oh, the nurse just said doctor," Dr. Wolf said disapprovingly and then continued her update with the typical analytical detachment of a trauma surgeon. "Well, the good news is that he has a will to live that I haven't really seen before. The bad news is that the injuries he has sustained are quite severe. The impact should have killed him, and he was very lucky the Orthopedic Surgeons were there to stabilize him."

My mother took a moment to let that sink in and then asked the question she has been dreading since she talked with Steve. "Will my son live, Doctor?"

"It is too soon to tell." Dr. Wolf replied bluntly. "Trauma cases we see like this have a 95% mortality rate. We immediately ran into problems with intubation, and I had to perform an emergency tracheotomy as soon as he got into the OR. Life support is keeping him alive right now. We have removed his spleen and are currently sewing up the perforations in his intestines. He has also developed a blood clot in his arm and one in his leg. We have put him on the maximum dosage of blood thinners to combat the clots."

"Is there any good news?" my mother asked weakly.

"He is still alive, and he is still fighting," Dr. Wolf said. "Most patients in his shape don't make it this far. I have to go back into the OR, but I wanted to update you on his condition."

As soon as Dr. Wolf left the waiting room, my mother went to the ladies room and threw up. Being the former wife of a doctor, she told me she thought I was going to die that night. Everything that she had seen and heard led her to believe she was being prepared for the worst outcome. After several more hours of surgery, Dr. Wolf came back out to give my mother another update.

"We have just closed your son up and moved him up to Trauma ICU. He is on the critical watch list right now," Dr. Wolf told her. "He is still alive, but has now developed a fever, and we believe he is developing pneumonia. The next 24 hours are going to be critical to his survival."

"Thank you for working so hard to save my son's life doctor," my mother managed. Once Dr. Wolf left the waiting room, my mother ran back to the bathroom and was sick again.

Over the next two days, things went from bad to worse.

I developed a fever that went over 105 degrees and was literally burning my organs up; they put ice packs on my body to keep my temperature down. The second day, I developed Acute Respiratory Distress Syndrome, and they put me in a bed that would help rotate my body so I could breathe. Once you develop ARDS, there is a 50% mortality rate. Those odds didn't even take into consideration all the other complications I was facing.

While there were a lot of people praying for me, no one thought I would make it, and there was already talk of what to do once I passed. As I slipped in between this world and the next, I saw a lot of things that made me reflect upon the life I had lived.

What happens next is very difficult to explain and even more difficult for me to talk about. When you're in a coma, you are not supposed to dream. But I did! At least that is what I thought it was at first...

I started out in a constricted space that felt like a tiny sleeping bag. I could barely move around in it, and I was surrounded by a rhythmic sound like a heartbeat. I couldn't really see, but I felt as if I was in some type of womb surrounded by its tissue; I could feel the muted energy of the organic material around me.

Am I in a woman's womb, waiting to be born? I wondered as I tried to move around.

From inside this womb, I could only see a dull reddish light. The only way to describe it is to look directly at the sun with your eyes closed. That's what I was seeing when suddenly I felt terror and a sharp pain in my back. It felt like something was stabbing me as I frantically tried to move away from the pain.

In an instant, I was pulled out of there, and when I could open my eyes, I was floating through the sky. I floated across a vast area in the clouds where trees and mountains zipped by at a dizzying speed until they gave way to a massive field covered with lush vegetation and colors that were so vibrant, it was as if they were glowing. I pushed on further, flying through the air as I started to see signs of civilization. Massive cities seemed to float unsupported as people floated to and from places in this community.

At that moment, I felt a type of joy and peace that I had never experienced before and knew instinctively I would be safe.

From there, I was transported to different places in time itself, jumping ahead in the life of my loved ones. I saw my sister and her husband, but they were older now, surrounded by their family and friends, enjoying their full lives. There was such a sense of joy in my heart as I saw the ones who loved me happy and fulfilled.

I quickly flashed forward from that moment and saw the end of days. The initial joy and peace I felt were quickly replaced with an indescribable terror and dread. It is the most frightening thing I have ever seen, and I am not prepared to talk about that yet.

Then I was transported to a communal place to live and was greeted by my niece. The feeling of love combined with community immediately returned and I felt safe again. My niece was two years old at the time of my crash, but here, she looked to be 11 or 12. She had long blond flowing hair, and I instantly recognized her.

"Hi, David, I am going to show you around," she said as she took my hand. The warmth of her love and kindness surged through my body the instant she touched my hand, and I felt lighter and at peace. I noticed we were floating off the ground and when I looked over at her, she radiated a kind of compassion and empathy that seemed to shimmer off of her body.

As we started to float past different structures and people, I was having a hard time understanding her when she spoke. While I knew she was trying to help me, her language was much more evolved than mine. Her words were familiar, but I understood them more as concepts and ideas, as opposed to actual words.

She would say words like "Love, Kindness, Compassion, Peace, Tolerance" as if she were trying to have a conversation with me. I realized very quickly that she was trying to dumb things down for me so that I would understand her.

The good news was that the longer I was with her, the more I started to understand what she was saying.

I knew enough at this point to realize I was in transition – or already dead. If this was a dream, it felt like the longest dream ever. I realized that something must have happened to me because I was conscious that these surroundings did not exist in my world. We would pass waterfalls that had no beginning or end; they just floated in the middle of the sky in a state of infinity.

At first, I panicked a little when I came to the realization that I had died, but then I became very comfortable with the idea that I had made the transition. I felt my time on earth was done, and I began to embrace this new world.

While I don't remember a lot of it, I do remember that everyone seemed perfectly content in their lives. We would float from place to place, meeting people and I soon realized I was actually meeting their souls in human form. I noticed a bright light, almost like a Halo, surrounded their bodies.

I could literally read the light that radiated off of them.

It was as if every action, every word, and every idea that the person ever had or would have radiated off of their entire body. The longer I was there, the more I was able to read what was radiating off of them and understand what they were saying. I began to understand the greater concepts they were trying to teach me and realized they were preparing me for the final transition.

As time wore on, I found myself reading the Halo around them while they spoke, often paying more attention to it than the person speaking to me.

"It is considered rude to read a person's Halo when you are speaking with them, David," my niece gently admonishes me. "It is a sign that you still cannot trust them."

"I am sorry, it is just...so amazing," I tell her. "Being able to meet a stranger and within a couple of minutes know them better than their spouse would after 50 years of marriage. I have never felt this connected, but I will try not to do it anymore."

"It's alright, most people in transition do it," she says kindly. "I just knew you would want to be aware of it, but don't worry. As long as you do what feels right to you here, you will thrive."

"What do I do for a job?" I ask her as we continue to float through the cities.

"Whatever you want to do. We all complete each other here," she replies. "Don't worry. I will be here to guide you as long as you need me."

"Thank you," I tell her with a profound gratitude in my voice. One of the other things I have noticed is that every time someone said, "Thank you," or expressed a feeling I actually felt what the person was saying. It gave the words "Thank you," new meaning as I actually felt their gratitude.

I have never felt so connected, loved, understood or appreciated in my entire life.

There were no glaring inequities and everyone was happy and peaceful. While people looked normal, you could travel in an instant to wherever you thought of in your mind. In this world, greed, violence, inequality and intolerance simply did not exist, which was the opposite of what I saw at the end of days. I finally had found a place I belonged and was totally accepted and loved.

I was home, in my mind.

A moment later, I was standing with my niece in front of a brilliant white tunnel that was swirling with energy. That energy was pulling me towards it, and I was so eager to experience it. It was as if every love, every joy, every happiness I have ever felt was beckoning me. I realized it was time for me to transition and make my choice.

It was almost impossible to resist, but as powerfully drawn as I was to the tunnel, something in my soul was holding me back. I had the innate feeling that my time on Earth was not done, and I needed to stay on it to protect my nephew.

This confused me because Kyle and Veronica were the most loving and protective parents I knew. I also felt guilty, because I loved my niece and nephew equally and didn't understand why I wasn't drawn to protect her as well... but there was no doubt that I was being drawn to protect my nephew by something just as strong as the light.

I knew it was my soul's choice to make and in that instant, I made my decision.

Suddenly, I was back in the hospital bed. I was transported there in the blink of a thought. I could hear the machines and sounds of the hospital. My eyes started to open, and they stung; I hadn't used them in over three weeks. I felt both disappointment and relief that I had made the decision to come back.

All of the love, happiness and compassion disappeared, and it was replaced with an incredible exhaustion and physical pain.

Later, once my eyes were adjusted to being used again, I noticed a steady stream of people visiting the room directly across the hall from mine. Family and friends were visiting an elderly woman; they were saying good bye to her. I could tell she had a profound effect on the people in her life, and that made me think of the life I had been living.

By writing this book, I have talked about some of my darkest secrets, and I have shared things I never thought I would share with anyone. There is still one thing I have never told anyone. I'll share it now. I warn you it sounds VERY flaky ... but it is what I saw.

When I first woke up from my coma, I saw a glow around each of the people around me, like a subtle (and sometimes not so subtle) light that literally radiated off the person's body. I was immediately reminded of the Halo I had seen during the time I crossed over.

However, I couldn't read this light; I could only see it.

At first, I thought it might be effects of the drugs that they had me on. I didn't tell anyone because I didn't want them to think I had a screw loose. It would take me a while to figure out what the light represented. As time went by it seemed to indicate who this person really was and how they felt at that moment.

The brighter the person's light, the better the person turned out to be.

The elderly woman dying across the hall from me was radiating a light that was intense and beyond bright. Like a shooting star, and I knew it was eventually going out, but before being extinguished, its intensity was almost blinding.

Everyone who visited this woman was affected by that light, and I saw it attached itself to them as they left. In a very real and visual way, I was witnessing the effects of a truly loving and compassionate person on their loved ones.

At that moment, more than anything in the world, I wanted to be that person in the lives of the people I loved most. I knew I had a long way to go before I could hope to achieve in my life all that she had, but I decided at that moment, *that* was the person I was going to be.

Later that night, the elderly woman passed on. Her light blinked out in an instant and rose to the ceiling and through it. As they wheeled her away and cleaned the room, I realized that I was the only person seeing these things. It was a deeply personal experience for me and made me realize how much our actions affect others.

I am convinced that she passed on with no regrets, having left this world a better place. I believe she knew she had touched those closest to her and that she had a profound effect on them. I never knew her name or saw her face, but she is one of my greatest inspirations; I wanted to do the same thing with my life.

Awake in the hospital, I started to go through the list of things I had done. Like my motorcycle accident, what I had allowed myself to get involved in emotionally was going to require a good deal of recovery. Every long journey starts with that first step, and lying in my bed I had taken mine.

The next morning I got a visit from the physical therapist and my first reality check: I was in really bad shape, physically. The ventilator that I was hooked up to had been providing over 95% of my air intake. I wasn't strong enough to breathe on my own and just thinking about doing something – something as simple as sitting up in bed – was exhausting.

I had been in bed for about 29 days and dropped close to 40 pounds, thanks to what I now call "The Coma Diet."

In addition to the ventilator hose attached to my throat, I had a central line running four different racks of drugs directly into my heart, a chest tube inserted into my body, and fifty-five staples holding my stomach together. As soon as the physical therapist walked into the room, he asked me to get out of bed and stand up.

"I want to, buddy, but it may take a moment to get me there," I croaked.

"I will help you up, but the sooner you get out of bed, the sooner you can start walking again," he said as they adjusted the ventilator so I could move. I tried to stand up, but my legs were too weak. I had lost a lot of muscle as well as weight, and my legs were half their normal size. The physical therapist decided I wasn't pushing myself hard enough.

"Come on! You need to try harder," he told me as I started to falter. "You can do this."

"I get what you are trying to do," I wheezed and took a second to catch my breath, as I sat back down on the bed, "but you have to understand I am going to push myself harder than any other patient you have. When I say I can't do it, I really can't do it physically. It isn't a mental thing."

"I know what I am doing," he replied defensively. "You can push yourself harder."

"Let's try again tomorrow," I told him as I start to get back into bed. The room was spinning, and I just didn't trust this guy. He had a kind of darkness around him that made me a little wary.

The physical therapist wasn't a bad guy, but he seemed to consider compassion a kind of weakness; he was only interested in getting results. I knew I needed someone who understood that I would push myself as hard as I could, but I didn't need to be "toughened up."

The following day, I got another physical therapist, and we got on the same page before we started. His "light" was much brighter, and I ended up achieving a lot that day. He kept on trying to slow me down, but I wanted to get out of the hospital as quickly as possible.

I was amazed by the compassion and tireless dedication of everyone at the hospital and everything they did to get me better. In a weird way, after years of neglect, I was given the chance to see another side of people on this planet. I had become so convinced that the world was made up of people that were only focused on themselves and everything revolved around money, power, sex and violence. Here, they were only interested in healing me.

At the hospital, I was surrounded by a lot of bright light. I soaked it up.

Four days after I woke up, my father visited me.

I had been desperate to see him. He was still my father, warped as he was, and I longed for the security, sense of safety and comfort of having him there with me. However, that changed the second he arrived and what I saw frightened me.

The moment he came into the room, I wanted him to leave.

"Johnny's" eyes were looking at me, not my father's. He was trying to be upbeat, but I could tell he was disappointed. I began to imagine what that disappointment meant. Instead of a kind of light, all I could see was this terrible darkness surrounding him. It reminded me of what I saw at The End of Days.

Instead of feeling comforted by my father's presence, I feared for my life.

I had seen "Johnny" operate long enough to know I was now a liability in his eyes. A lot of machines and switches were keeping me alive, and I realized any life, even mine, meant nothing to him, especially if it threatened his happiness or his financial relationship with my grandma.

I couldn't let him know that I saw this, or that I was that scared. I was lying there, immobile, in desperate pain, connected to tubes and alone with him in my room. I knew I couldn't defend myself.

I have never felt more helpless in my life, and it was terrifying.

"I just want you to know we haven't told your grandmother what happened," he says as soon as he walks in the door. "We were afraid it would kill her."

"No problem, I understand. Are the girls here?" I croak back as I try desperately to keep the fear out of my voice.

"No," he replies quickly. "But they know. They feel bad that they didn't come to see you, but they are going to call you later."

"I understand," I say immediately. I would have sworn that the sky was purple if that made him happy. The darkness is literally radiating off of him, and I start to wonder if the painkillers I am on are making me hallucinate.

He sits down in a chair next to the bed and starts watching HBO GO, killing time until he can go. I know he is counting the minutes until he could get out of here, and it is the longest hour of my life. As he gets up from the chair, the darkness seemed to stick to it a little. Like the darkness somehow stained the fabric of the chair.

When he leaves, the darkness leaves with him and stain on the chair eventually evaporates. I breathe a sigh of relief. I think about what I just saw and dismiss it.

It has to be the drugs I am on, I reassure myself as I fall asleep. *I am just seeing things.*

I did occasionally talk to my father on the phone after that, and those conversations were helpful. He gave me insight as to what shape I was in. He had talked with the surgeon who checked up on me every day to get progress reports on my condition and how the antibiotics were working. He played the part of the doctor, and I was grateful for the information.

His second visit was shorter than the first, but the drugged-out effect had worn off, and I was now seeing things very clearly.

Unfortunately, the darkness around my father didn't go away. It intensified. The second he entered the room, everything grew a little darker. The best way to describe what I saw is to think of what the heat haze coming out of a jet engine looks like or the shimmer you see on a hot road during the summer, but slightly darker.

They had removed the ventilator hose from my throat that day, and one of my other doctors, Dr. Hansen is cutting the gangrene out of my neck hole where the tube had been inserted. Dr. Hansen is talking with my father while he makes his cuts.

"The hole in the throat should close in about three weeks on its own," Doctor Hansen tells him as he makes another cut. "We put steri-strips on to make sure nothing gets in there."

"It closes naturally with no sutures?" my father asks.

"Yes, the skin instinctively grows over the hole. No suture are needed." Doctor Hansen replies.

At that moment, I look over at my father and realize he is observing the procedure with no emotion. He looks down quickly as if he knows he is supposed to show *some* type of sympathetic response to seeing this happening to his son and has been caught failing to imitate the appropriate emotional response.

Both times my father has visited me; I have noticed not only the darkness around him but that he has displayed no emotional reaction to what has happened to me. After five more minutes of cutting out the gangrene, Dr. Hansen puts on the steri-strips and leaves.

"Well, it looks like you're going to get out of here without a scratch," he says once Dr. Hansen leaves the room.

Is that regret in his voice? I wonder and then it hits me. *He really is disappointed that I didn't die in the accident; it isn't just in my head!*

He spends another ten minutes in the room and then he leaves. As usual, the darkness leaves with him, and I start to relax. I try not to think about what I just saw or my father's disappointment. As usual, I try and defend his actions.

If he didn't care about me, then why did he bother visiting me in the hospital? I wonder, as try to convince myself I am wrong in my assumptions.

It took me a couple of days to understand that my father's visit and concern had nothing to do with me or my health and recovery. It was, like all of his public actions, an act. He wanted to be able to tell my grandmother he was at my bedside in case I died. While this thought saddened me – *and again I felt guilty for questioning my father's love – this time, it felt true.*

In that hospital bed, with nothing to do but think, I wondered about the darkness that surrounded my father. Maybe I wasn't seeing things. Maybe it had always been there, but like "Johnny Russell," I hadn't been ready to see it yet. I started to analyze all of the things I overlooked in the past because he was my father. The things he said and the way he looked at me then ... and now.

I was reminded of the night in Montreal when my father's "girlfriend" was a no show. He tried to find me but didn't know "which" strip club I was at. The next morning, he complained, "I went looking for you, but couldn't find you. I've never felt so alone and unhappy in my entire life." I knew I had heard that line some place before, but didn't think too much about it. I managed a quick, "Sorry about that; it won't happen again!"

But he jogged my memory completely when he used the same line two days later on the "girlfriend" he was supposed to meet: *I've never felt so alone and unhappy in my entire life.* I instantly remembered where I had heard it before: he said that exact same thing to Maria when he lost the custody case, and his father passed away. It had served him well over the years, so he continued to use it.

On his wife, on me, on prostitutes...

While it was emotionally devastating to finally accept who my father really was, I was fortunate enough to be surrounded by the selfless physicians, nurses, physical therapists, and technicians that worked at the hospital. They reminded me that there are good people out there; you just have to look for them. Toward the end of my stay in the hospital, several of them showed up at my room individually to thank me.

"Shouldn't I be thanking you?" I asked the first nurse who came to my room. She had just told me that she was one of the nurses in the Trauma OR when they operated on me.

"You can always thank us, but let me explain what I am talking about," she says in the same patient and kind tone that I have grown accustomed to at this hospital. "Have you ever seen the movie *Groundhogs Day*?"

"Yes," I say as I start to wonder where she is going with this.

"Normally when a patient comes in as bad a shape as you were in, they die," she says in a matter of fact tone. "No matter what life-saving measures we try, the patient eventually flatlines. After that happens, 30 or 40 or 50 times in a row, you begin to lose hope like Bill Murray did in the movie."

I keep waiting for her to make her joke, but realize she isn't kidding and blurt out, "That has to be so depressing for you guys."

"You have no idea. A lot of nurses switch out of Trauma Surgery because of it. It just becomes too depressing and demoralizing for us," she says but then smiles. "But you living and walking out of here reminds us that it's still possible to save someone in a critical condition like yours! It gives us the hope we need to keep going."

"I don't know what to say, but I am happy if my walking out of here helps you guys in any way," I say quickly. "I also want to thank you for taking such great care of me and I think if anyone deserves a thank you, it is you guys and not me."

We talked for a while, and then she went on her way, but others would soon follow with the same message. It reminded me how lucky I was to live through the accident, and it made me even more determined to make sure my future actions would reflect my appreciation for the second chance I had been given.

Each person at the hospital had a different story describing how they helped me, and I thanked them as best I could. I recognized the irony that at my most vulnerable, darkest time, during which I suffered so much pain, those weeks in the hospital reaffirmed my faith that there are good people out there.

As I started to recover, I realized I hadn't checked in on my business, and there were a number of things in play. First up was the green light on a low budget film I was producing. Because of Facebook, most of the people I dealt with knew about the accident, so my not returning phone calls and moving things along business-wise was excused. I was the guy who normally returned a phone call the day I got it, even when I was drinking. It was time to get back to work.

I called the director of my low budget film first.

The director and line producer knew about my accident and had picked up the slack in my absence. When I talked with Alan, the director, he told me everything was fine, and the film was set to start shooting in a couple of weeks. I knew Eric my line producer was also helping Alan, which made me relax a little when Alan told me everything was going great.

"Just concentrate on your recovery, David. Everything is fine, with the film," Alan said, and his kind voice resonated over the phone and gave me a sense of assurance.

All of my clients were booked out and taken care of, as I had planned on being busy with the shoot. I figured I could breathe a little bit and just take a reduced credit and fee on Alan's film. What I needed was time and rest so I could get better.

But that wasn't meant to be.

CHAPTER NINE

WHO HAS TIME FOR RECOVERY?

Thirty-two days after my accident, I left the hospital.

Most of the physicians and nurses were surprised that I was being released as early as I was, but my determination to get out of there, plus their fear that I would catch something at the hospital, had been factored into the final decision.

Physically, I was still in pretty bad shape. The 2-inch long hole in my throat was just starting to close, and I had to use a walker due to the muscle loss in my legs. I could only walk 30 feet before both the pain, and physical exhaustion overwhelmed me.

Mentally, I was sifting through a mountain of emotions and new information. The kindness and compassion I had been shown at the hospital by the doctors, nurses, physical therapist and technician had shined a spotlight on the fact there are good people in this world that were worthy of my trust. I kept thinking about what my physical therapist James told me on my third day of physical therapy.

"You know, you are the tenth patient I have worked with that has died and come back," he tells me as we use my walker to navigate down the hallway.

"What were the others like?" I ask him and stop walking for a second to catch my breath.

"Each one was a little different, but they all made huge changes in their lives," he tells me. "Once they left the hospital, each of them realized how every day should be valued and not just taken for granted."

"Weren't they doing that before they got here?" I ask.

"No," he says as he looks me right in the eyes. "They were just trying to get to the goal line, and forgot to enjoy the journey of getting there."

"What do you mean?" I ask.

Along with Dr. Hansen, James was someone I really tried to pay attention to while I was at the hospital. He was a 29-year-old ex-pro football player who looked like a smaller version of The Rock. While he didn't look like the type of guy to share profound life lessons, I quickly learned his job had given him some unique insights on life.

"They got so caught up in accomplishing their goals; they didn't take the time to enjoy the life they were living," he says as he starts to connect the dots for me. "From what you have told me, it sounds like you have done the same thing."

"I guess you have a point there," I say casually, but his words hit me like a ton of bricks. I had never taken the time to really appreciate the life I was living, even before I met "Johnny Russell." Having been raised to believe that life had no meaning until you reached some type of marker of success, I never took the time to enjoy mine. In my mind, I had to achieve all of my goals before I could enjoy the fruits of my labor.

This belief was constantly reinforced by my father.

Talking with James made me start to realize that my entire life had meaning and purpose; regardless of where I was on the road toward accomplishing my goals. I had learned that life is extraordinarily fragile and to take joy in accomplishing even the simplest goals in life.

You never know when this gift of life can be taken from you.

It was during this time; I started to really open myself up to the wisdom of others. I had been raised to be cynical and look for the worst in people, with the sole exception being my family. I started to re-evaluate a lot of the core philosophies I had been raised to believe in. I knew I had to make a lot of changes in the way I was living my life, if I was ever going to be truly happy.

My immediate problem was getting my health and strength back, something I had always taken for granted. I stayed at my mother and stepfather's house during the first month of my recovery. I owe them a great deal for taking me in and helping me get my strength back.

The first day at their house, I got a call from my father and it was a perfect example of what I grew up with. The hospital that saved me was a Catholic hospital, and he wanted to make sure I didn't pay them for whatever my health insurance didn't cover.

"You need to pay Dr. Hansen as soon as possible," my father tells me. "He is a good doctor and deserves to be paid. Tell him to put his invoice in the system immediately, but I don't want you to pay the hospital."

"Why wouldn't I pay the hospital?" I ask. "They saved my life!"

"Use your brain, David. It is a Catholic hospital," he says. "After all the Catholics have put me through, I can't believe you would even ask me that question."

"But they saved *my* life," I argue. "Wouldn't you want me to pay them for that?"

"Just do what I tell you to do," he says angrily, acting as if I am betraying him somehow. "I thought if anyone would understand why they shouldn't be paid; it would be my own son."

"I am not trying to start a fight, Dad. I am just trying to understand your reasoning," I say calmly. "I know you don't like the church, but there are a lot of good people that work at that hospital. I wouldn't be alive if it weren't for all of their hard work."

"I don't have time for this, and I have a patient waiting for me," he says angrily. "Just don't pay them!"

A second later I realize he has hung up the phone. I start to call him back like I always do, but then stop. I think about James, Dr. Hansen and everyone else at the hospital. After a moment, I hang up the phone.

The second day I was at my mom's house, I got a call from our production lawyer Bob about the film I was producing. I had pretty much decided since things were going so well in pre-production, I was going to sit this one out and take the time to really recover. This call would drastically alter that plan.

"I hate to lay this on you right after you got out of the hospital, but I don't think the film is going to happen unless you come back immediately," Bob tells me as soon as he was finished telling me how happy he was that I was still alive.

"What are you talking about?" I ask as I am not sure I have heard him correctly. "I talked to Alan just before I got out of the hospital, and he told me everything was fine."

"He hasn't hired any of the actors yet," Bob says flatly.

"You're kidding, right?" I ask thirty seconds later. It takes me that long to process what is happening because I can't believe he is telling me the truth.

"It's not quite as bad as it sounds," Bob tells me calmly. "Alan has sat down with Kelly and Michael, but hasn't made a final decision regarding either of them yet."

"Why hasn't he pulled the trigger?" I ask him frantically. "We are a week and a half away from the start of principal photography!"

"Really? You know I hadn't thought about that," Bob says sarcastically and then brings me up to speed. "I have tried to push him to make a decision, but every time I ask him about making an offer, he tells me he is still thinking about it."

"If this is some type of joke, Bob, you need to stop right now," I say, but when he doesn't respond, I realize this isn't a joke. "This is really happening, isn't it?"

"I wouldn't joke about something like this!" Bob says defensively. "I am not the producer, and there is only so far I can push for an answer. If this is going to happen, I need to start their deals yesterday."

As a deal maker, I knew exactly where he was.

Directors make the casting decisions in consultation with the producer. Then the producer and the lawyers make the deal happen. The problem is once you make an offer, their side (the actors' agents, lawyers, managers and the artist themselves) decide if they want to take it. The back and forth on some negotiations can take months.

We had a week to close the deals for the entire cast.

Further, you have other actor-oriented departments on standby waiting to see who you hire. A costume designer can't properly fit actors for their wardrobes, until you hire them and get their sizes. That is just one department. When any department is on standby, there is a domino effect on everything in the production of the film. The longer you wait, and the less prep you have and the more it's going to cost you.

We were rapidly approaching the line where we were going to have to push the film's start date back. The problem with that was the network wanted it in a compressed time frame, and Alan was already pushing back against the idea of getting it to them in that short of a time period.

The director, steering the ship and actualizing his vision, has a huge responsibility. He relies on guys like the producer to make sure he doesn't have to worry about the minutiae of deal making, etc. I knew that Alan was used to having others handle that stuff, and without a hands-on Producer, we were in trouble.

It was time for me to go back to work.

It was Friday afternoon, and I did some quick mental calculations about what I would be physically able to do. I had made some pretty good progress in the hospital; I could walk the length of the corridor, with my walker, before I was winded. But I knew I couldn't bring my walker into the pre-production office! That visual would kill any chance of me being able to do my job!

I had to stand on my own two feet.

"I'll be in the production office this Tuesday, and I'll make some calls now to get the ball rolling. We can make the date!" I told Bob. I hung up the phone and called Jessica, the writer, and confirmed everything he has just told me. She was an Associate Producer on the film and was in the production office.

Alan and I had sold the project. We brought Jessica in as the writer and developed the script from scratch. She wrote the script and, like Alan, she was also a friend and client. If it were just a money thing, I would have walked; I was really that exhausted and weak. However, we had sold the network the three of us working together, and everyone had a lot riding on this project. I couldn't let my friends down or the people that are financing the film.

I called Dr. Hansen and told him what I was about to do. After telling me I shouldn't do it, and knowing I would do it, with or without his input, he reluctantly agreed to help. My main question was how do I manage the physical exhaustion?

"That's the pain, and what it is doing to your body," Dr. Hansen explained. "Take your pain pills." He correctly suspected that I hadn't been taking them.

He knew how frightened I was of becoming addicted to the pills because of my alcoholism. He had confronted me in the hospital when I had refused to take my pain meds after I got out of surgery and convinced me to trust him. What he didn't know was my real reason for trusting him.

Since I had come out of the coma, every time I saw him, an intense bright light always surrounded him. He seemed to be the exact opposite of my father; a good man devoted to the welfare of others. When he asked me why I wasn't taking the pain medication, I told him the truth and didn't try to cover up my alcoholism.

I was learning there were good people in this world.

"David, I am your doctor, and you are under my care. I am not going to let you become addicted to anything," Dr. Hansen told me, but I guess he saw hesitation in my eyes because he went on to say, "If you don't take the medicine it will hinder your recovery. All of your vitals are elevating because you aren't taking the medicine. You have to trust me!"

Asking people for help and trusting them has always been difficult for me. I had been raised to see all the potential liabilities of trusting someone. At every turn, I was reminded of the high price my father had paid for trusting someone and starting a family. This was one of the reasons it took me a year and a half to reach out to Margaret for help, and why I was still single.

What I had learned from my time in the hospital was that not everyone had an agenda like my father led me to believe. Dr. Hansen, James and the others that worked at the hospital were not in it for the money like my father, but true healers. In the hospital, I started to learn it was alright to ask others for help and trust them.

I realized I just had to be more careful of *who* I asked for help and trusted.

Trusting Dr. Hansen was the first step I took in trusting people outside of my family. We came up with a plan to manage the pain at night, and I would gut it out during the day when I was working on the film.

"Just because your wounds are starting to scab up, doesn't mean the internal injuries have completely healed, and you are doing this against my advice as your doctor," Dr. Hansen warned me.

Knowing I didn't have a choice; I came up with my plan on how to fool people in production to thinking I was okay. Trusting my doctor was one thing, but I knew I couldn't appear weak to my production crew.

My biggest concern at that point was ditching the walker and not collapsing in front of my crew. I came up with a plan to mask my pain and build up my strength for what I was facing.

I call the next month and a half "extreme physical therapy."

Friday night, I started my training by trying to stand without the walker for ten minutes at a time. That didn't go so well. I fell a couple of times and wasn't able to stand on my own for more than three minutes at a time. Also, I was getting dizzy and sweating a lot. By the time I got into bed that night I was exhausted, but I felt like I made some progress.

Saturday was my first attempt at walking without the walker. I made sure my mother wasn't around when I tried this because I had a feeling I would be falling a lot, and I was right. I quickly became adept at looking for things to stabilize me in case I started to get light headed. I began to be able to anticipate when this was going to happen, and I realized if I stopped moving and took a breath, it went away.

Sunday, I finally mastered walking 50 steps, taking a moment to regain my strength, and then walking 50 more steps. Like so much of my life, I don't recommend anyone try this. Stay in bed and don't be stupid. You can really hurt yourself when you push your recovery!

Monday, I wasn't sweating quite as much, and I learned that if I leaned against something, my strength returned a lot faster. I had talked with most of the people in production and I let everyone know I was back in the office on Tuesday. I was comfortable enough sitting that I knew I could pull it off, but only if I paced myself and used the 50-step technique I came up with.

Tuesday morning, I discovered that our pre-production office was on the second floor of a building without an elevator. It was 380 steps from the car to the office. The staircase in the office was my Mount Everest, and I made sure I always walked up it alone. I didn't want people to see me gasping for air as I clung to the railing.

I did come up with a trick that no one noticed and, in retrospect, turned out to be a great way to produce a film. I would walk to one person in the office, asking them a question about something going on in their department relating to the film. I would keep talking to that person, regaining my strength, until someone else would walk into my line of sight. If that person were on the way to where I was going, I would call out their name and ask them to wait a second, "I have a question about..."

This gave me the opportunity to walk to them (and eventually my ultimate destination) without appearing to catch my breath.

I hoped I looked like an engaged and on-top-of-things producer, and not a guy about to collapse.

Everyone was extremely understanding in pre-production and the shoot itself. More often than not, I think people did what I asked not just because I was the boss, but in the words of one grip, "Who is going to argue with a guy who was just in a coma and died twice?!"

Still, I came close to passing out during the first day. We were on a location scout in the mountains, and it was about 107 degrees. Our line producer Eric looked at me as I was trying to walk up the hill to where we were planning to shoot. Eric is a great guy and was more than a little concerned about me.

"Hey buddy, you look like you're about to pass out!" Eric called out to me. I was about fifty yards behind him trying to catch my breath.

"I can handle it, Eric. Just give me a second," I wheezed.

"You're as white as a sheet," he said, and I could hear the concern in his voice. "Maybe you should wait in the car while we go up the hill? Trust me. I can handle this."

When I looked closely at him, I realized he was surrounded by a faint white light. I decided to trust his instincts and agreed to sit this one out. "You know, Eric, that may not be such a bad idea."

When I got back to the car, I realized I was soaked with sweat and quickly turned on the air-conditioning. The car was spinning, and I was getting vertigo by just sitting there. My heart was racing as I tried to catch my breath. In trying to push through the pain of climbing the trail, I didn't realize how close I came to passing out. I was very lucky Eric was there for me, and I thanked him when he got back to the car.

From that moment on, I really started to pay attention to the light surrounding the people on this shoot. Whenever I saw that bright white light, I knew that person was trying to help me. While I didn't see it as frequently as I did in the hospital, I learned to trust those people, and it served me well throughout filming.

It was a 16-day shoot on a budget of under a million dollars; we ran a car off a cliff, staged a fight scene in which we threw an actor off a cliff, and the script called for three characters to die. We were trying for too much at that budget and pushing too hard.

Luckily, there were so many good people who helped me get through this difficult shoot.

Our leading lady was one of them. She had also had a near death experience; in fact, she went through something a lot tougher than I had to endure. We talked about how this type of experience changes you. We both agreed that it sharpens your perspective and makes you really want to make every day count.

I was constantly reminded of how kind people can be by experiencing the crew's simple acts of kindness. It was the little things, like Jessica greeting me with a special green drink every morning to boost my energy. I tried to show my gratitude to all involved in that shoot by doing everything I could to make their jobs easier and more comfortable.

From the second you start shooting a film, you spend an obscene amount of money every day, and if you're a Producer, you stop sleeping. On average, I got about 4 hours sleep a night, and I started falling asleep in the shower before going to bed. Every waking minute, you're thinking of the next shot, the next setup, the next hurdle – all while trying to keep everyone happy.

Of course, when you have a lot of artistic personalities on a set, you have to be adept at reading all of them and know when to step in and when to step back.

Our Director of Photography was a good case in point. He was a total perfectionist and got us some really great stuff. Some people would complain that he was going for too much, but I always backed him because I knew that although he might be exacting, his vision was solid, and his intentions were good. He also was surrounded by the white light, but of course, I never shared that fact with anyone, on set or off.

One of the good things about my covering my inability to walk more than 50 steps without being winded was that I got to know everyone on set. Being that connected as a producer gave the crew instant access to me when there was a problem or concern. Always talking to someone involved with the production of the film allowed me to avoid quite a few disasters.

I am reminded of our second week of shooting. A grip that I had befriended came to me on behalf of the crew and asked for my help.

"Listen, this isn't a money thing, it is a sleep thing, we are just doing too much with too little time and the heat is killing us," the grip said sincerely. Since I left the hospital, I had decided I would be 100 percent honest in everything I did from the second I left there.

"You're right. We didn't schedule enough time on this one because we don't have the money," I said, and he couldn't mask his shocked expression as I continued, to be honest with him. "I can't change the schedule, but once we move to Malibu, I promise we will slow down. I know you guys are doing too much, and it is our fault as producers."

Normally this type of interaction doesn't happen with a producer and a grip. There is a chain of command in place and everyone talks to their department head. Also, a less experienced producer (Me) would never admit to making a mistake, but would try and turn it around on the crew making it their fault. In other words, pull a manipulation tactic like my father.

Luckily, I had found out I was not my father's son.

Also, I noticed early in the shoot that the grip had that same type of light coming from him that Eric and our director of photography had. I decided again to be 100% honest with him as I asked for his help.

"Can you give me two more days of this before we slow down?" I asked him.

"Two days, but after that, we have to slow down. Half the crew already wants to quit," he told me as he started to walk back to work, but then turned back to me. "Thanks for being honest, at least."

Throughout my life, I have worked every job from construction to running my own business, and the one thing I have learned is that if you hire good people, they will always want to do the best job they can. Sometimes it's simply enough to acknowledge the challenges that they are facing, *even if you can't fix them.*

The last day was the biggest day of the shoot and the one on which we spent the most money. We were going to shoot two stunts where any sane production would shoot only one. For the first stunt, we attached a wire to one of our stuntmen and threw him off a cliff after a staged fight scene. It worked but took a lot of time.

Too much time.

We were then planning to shoot the car flying off the cliff at dusk ("magic hour") so we would not have to light the car crash, which was supposed to take place at night. Magic hour is that perfect light before sunset where you have a window of 30 minutes to shoot something before the sun disappears. Unfortunately, we had to set everything back up at the bottom of the hill, where the stunt was supposed to take place. That was the plan, anyway, but as is the norm in movie making, we started to fall behind schedule. It wasn't anyone's fault.

By the time we wrapped up the scene on the top of the hill, everyone was scrambling down the hill to set up the final shot. When we got to the location, it was already magic hour, and people were literally running to set up the five cameras to record the shot. We weren't sure we were going to be able to set up all of the cameras in time.

That's when we ran into problem number two.

In setting up the car to go over the cliff, its engine, transmission, etc. had been removed. Unfortunately, the battery had also been removed as well, and that meant no headlights. Everyone started throwing out ideas as the sun faded behind the mountain. Should we grab a battery from someone else's car? Attach mini-maglites to the headlight sockets? The sun began to set. The cameras were set up, but we had officially passed magic hour.

As a producer, I was in a lot of trouble.

To light the scene would take at least three hours, we were already into overtime, and I had a crew that already wanted to quit. To not light the scene and shoot it as is would get us the shot for the story, but it would look like garbage. This was the most expensive scene of the film, and I had to make the final call knowing the right decision could cost me everything.

My friend the grip was looking at me, along with the DP, the Director, Eric and the entire crew. I knew most of the crew would quit if I tried to force them to light the shot. I also knew that they took tremendous pride in their work and knew what was at stake. At that moment, I decided to take a leap of faith and trust my crew to do the right thing.

"OK," I said. "I guess we're just going to have to shoot it as is. It will take too long to light, and everyone is exhausted."

"It's going to look like absolute crap if we shoot it without lighting it!" the DP exploded as I anticipated. "This is the biggest scene of the film!"

The light surrounding the DP was now beyond bright, and I noticed that it was starting to spread throughout his entire department. With his reaction, I had just secured Camera and Electric to the cause of lighting the shot.

"It wouldn't take that long to light it," my friend the grip said while everyone stood around and his light started to spread to his department as well and his crew started to nod in agreement. "I bet we could do it in an hour."

"I can order some food too," Eric said as everyone looked at me to make the call.

"Well if you guys are cool with it, and we can do it safely, let's get to it," I said, once I knew I had everyone on board. "Everyone will get paid double overtime."

That night affirmed for me that whether you actually see the light like I did at the time, or people reveal themselves with their actions, there are good people out there if you just give them the chance to show you.

We got a beautiful shot that night, and it was all due to the crew being total pros and taking a great deal of pride in their work. They simply wanted to be acknowledged for the backbreaking work that they did, and I am the first to say, thank you. If memory serves, it didn't take one hour to light the shot properly. It took three. And they all knew that going in.

Total pros.

That night on the drive home, I thought of how my father would have handled this problem. I could see him saying, "If you want to get paid, hurry up and light this scene, otherwise you won't get paid at all." He would have used their livelihoods as a pressure point to bend them to his will.

In the past, I used to go to my father with my problems and ask him for advice. Now I found myself thinking about how he would handle something and I would do the exact opposite. The results I was getting with this contrary action were exactly the results I wanted.

I had finally realized my father's advice only benefited one person, *him.*

We shot the rest of the film on location on an estate in Malibu, and thanks to the cooler temperatures, the crew morale went up 100%. We made it through the last hurdle, on time and on budget.

My father finally checked in on me during the last week of shooting.

"I don't think we should tell your grandmother about you being in the accident," he says flatly. "It could kill her."

"I am getting tired of lying to grandma," I say without hesitation.

"What's that supposed to mean?" he asks.

"I understand keeping it from her when there was a chance I was going to die," I reply. "But I lived. I don't want to lie to grandma anymore. I will tell her in person, so she knows I am alright, but I am going to tell her."

"I don't want you telling your grandmother about the accident, period. This isn't up for debate!" he says angrily. "Haven't you already put this family through enough?"

"I am sorry if my having an accident upset people, but I am tired of lying all the time," I say flatly. "I just want to be honest with her."

"You are not going to say a word to her, and that is the end of this conversation!" he yells angrily and then hangs up.

At this point, as exhausted as I was, I very quickly came to the conclusion he was afraid I was going to tell her everything. I bought the motorcycles right after the "bonding" started, and he knew the hell he put me through. While I wasn't planning on telling my grandmother about "Johnny Russell" I had decided I wasn't going to enable my father anymore.

Since I had gotten out of the hospital, we had argued several times over the phone. The more I started to stand up for what I thought was the right thing to do, the more he began to threaten me and hang up the phone. What I realize now is that I had been enabling and covering for my father my entire life, even before I met "Johnny Russell."

A perfect example of this was the documentary I made on my grandmother several years before I "officially" met "Johnny Russell." My writer and director were editing when they ran into a problem and asked for my help.

"We have to talk about your father," the writer said. "We're listening to the audio and he doesn't sound human."

I started to laugh, but the director wouldn't let it go.

"We asked him a question about how he feels about his mother, and he sounds like he's talking about a car!" The director complains and then tells me. "He shows no warmth, no emotion! He sounds *sub-human*."

It didn't surprise me, I had seen some of the rough footage and knew there was a problem. Even back then, I tried to protect my father's image and make my father look good.

"Is there any way you can write something that will make him look better?" I asked and then give them an idea that I think will work. "Maybe some heartfelt dialogue that we can record of him and then play that over some of her racing footage or of them walking together?"

"I guess that would work," the director said begrudgingly.

With that idea in mind, the writer wrote out something appropriate and touching. It took about 30 takes over the phone, but my father eventually managed to record the audio without sounding like a soulless machine.

When I screened the documentary for my family, my grandmother was moved to tears as she told me, "I never knew he felt that way about me!" Of course, Maria tried to immediately kill my grandmother's moment of happiness.

"That doesn't even sound like something your father would say!" Maria snapped. While Maria knew my father wasn't capable of saying something this heartfelt, my grandmother didn't have a clue, and I smiled at both of them, not saying a word.

What's a small lie if it made Grandma that happy? I thought to myself at the time. *It was just a little lie.*

What I would find out later in life is those "little lies" add up over time. When my father had hung up on me this time, I started to wonder if I had done more harm than good in taking the high road to protect my family from the truth. How could my family protect themselves from "Johnny Russell," if they didn't know he existed?

I made the decision to tell my grandmother the truth about my accident. As much as it might have benefited me personally, I did decide to draw the line at telling her about "Johnny Russell," because I knew it might actually kill her. I decided I would just tell her about the accident and how it changed me, leaving out the rest of it. I would tell her in person, so she would know I was alright, but I wanted to be as honest as I could be with her.

Unfortunately, I would never get the chance.

CHAPTER TEN

THE WORLD LOSES AN ANGEL

Two weeks after that last phone call with my father, my grandmother died.

She had a massive aneurysm while she was driving and ran her car into the front of a 7-11. No pedestrians were hurt, but we would learn the world lost an angel. Anyone who was lucky enough to meet her would say that.

As soon as I heard my grandmother was in the hospital, I immediately flew back to Texas to be with her in her final days. Maria met me at the airport and quickly established the ground rules for my visit.

"Madison is taking what happened to Wanda very badly," she says as soon as I close the car door. "I hope you understand what a close relationship your sister had with her and will respect her wishes."

"Of course, I will, Maria," I tell her as I am genuinely worried about Madison and know this is a huge blow for her. She cared very deeply for my grandmother and was a huge source of joy in her life. I always felt better about my decision to stay away from the family, knowing she would be there to keep an eye on my grandmother.

"The rest of the family has decided to respect whatever requests Madison makes regarding your grandmother," she says as if she didn't hear me. "I know you are aware of how much your absence from the family upset your grandmother and that your sisters were the only ones there for her during that time."

"Maria, I get it," I say quickly trying to avoid another fight with her. "I understand Madison and Lisa were huge parts of Wanda's life, and I am not trying to take anything away from that. I am just thankful that they had the opportunity to make her happy."

"Good," she says coldly and turns over to look at me before she starts the car. "Because the last thing we need right now is you causing problems."

"I understand you feel protective of the girls right now, and I can assure you I didn't fly out here to cause any problems," I say calmly, but my stomach is twisting into a knot. "I came here to see my grandmother, and that is it. I can stay at grandma's house if that makes you feel any better."

"No," Maria says quickly. "Madison doesn't want anyone at the house. You can stay at my house as long as you promise to behave yourself."

With a massive effort, I manage to keep my mouth shut. I do this by reminding myself that Madison made my grandmother very happy. Although I had been raised to see the worst in people, I believe Madison did this with no other agenda in mind other than the fact she loved our grandmother.

If Madison had been anything like her mother, I would suspect her kindness was motivated by my grandmother telling each of us at family functions (unprompted) that when she passed, she was going to divide everything she had between us grandchildren – a third each. While I knew Maria valued money above everything else, I truly believed that Madison had a very genuine and loving relationship with my grandmother.

Of course, my grandma didn't play favorites with the children in the family; she loved us all equally. Considering the oil wells had been pumping since the early 80s, the amount of money she intended to leave us was substantial and every time she told us what she intended to do with her fortune, each of us would say thanks, but we would rather have her in our lives.

I knew my grandmother was worried about my sisters' financial future since both of my sisters had taken low paying jobs to give back to the community. She was as proud of them as I was and I know she wanted to make sure that they never had to worry about money.

Like the lady at the hospital who died the day I came out of my coma, my grandmother had a huge impact on everyone she had touched in her life. There was a steady stream of visitors, and Maria's entire family came to pay their last respects. The kindness and compassion Wanda practiced all of her life had clearly touched everyone she met.

I have spent countless nights trying to figure out how my father came from her, and I still haven't figured that one out.

Being inside another ICU again is deeply uncomfortable for me on many levels. Every alarm is an unpleasant reminder of my hospital stay several months ago, when each time I went to sleep, I wondered if I would wake up again. I had to walk outside every hour or so to relieve the stress I felt. Maria finally asked me where I was going, and I was dumb enough to tell her.

"Wow David, does everything have to be about you?" she says when I tell her how much the alarms bother me. "Try to think about someone else besides yourself for once. Remember we are here for your grandmother and to support Madison."

"I get that, Maria," I say calmly, but I realize she is starting to get to me. "That is why I didn't say anything to anyone and tried to be as subtle about it as possible."

"We are getting tired of having to text you every time someone comes to visit your grandmother," she says flatly. "They keep asking if you are here, and it is starting to upset Madison. You told me that you weren't going to be a problem."

"Maria, I am not trying to be a problem," I say defensively, but stop myself and realize that arguing with her is only going to upset my sisters and quickly change tactics. "Sorry. I will try and leave the room less."

"Just remember there are other people besides you that we have to think about," she says sternly. That is when I realize what is really upsetting her. People are asking about the "Bastard Son," and that is pulling focus from her grieving daughter in law act.

My father wasn't the only person that was disappointed when I didn't die. I think to myself as I see the anger in her eyes and a shiver runs down my spine. *I am really lucky I made it out of that hospital alive!*

As family and friends come to visit, they immediately remark at how much weight I have lost. After the second person asks me what diet I am on, I realize that my father and Maria haven't told anyone about my motorcycle accident.

Unbelievable. I think to myself. *I wonder if they would have told any-one if I died?*

With Maria sitting in Wanda's room playing the part of the grieving daughter-in-law, I start to ponder what Maria's next move will be. I realize that this is why she wants all of the focus in on Madison; that way there will be less chance of people finding out what happened to me.

Pretty soon she is going to ask me to keep my mouth shut. I think to myself, and I also realize I can't lie anymore. *Maria's family deserves better than that!*

Just as I couldn't figure out how my grandmother could give birth to and raise someone like my father; I was equally baffled by Maria's family. They were *really nice people* who treated me with kindness and love. When Maria's father Bernard asked me what diet I am on as I bump into him at the elevator, I quickly tell him the truth.

After a brief description of what happened, Bernard interrupts me.

"David, I have to tell you how sorry I am you went through all of that alone," he says tearfully. "If any of us had known, we would have flown out to be with you. I hope you can find it in your heart to forgive us."

"Bernard, there is nothing for me to forgive," I say quickly. "There was no way for you to know what happened."

"Maria and your father should have told us," he says angrily.

"Maybe they were worried someone would tell grandma what happened," I say, still trying to cover for my father, but my heart just isn't in it anymore.

"It isn't right, David," he says emotionally. "No one would have said anything, and they know that. The entire family should have been praying for you. I hope you know that is what we would have done if we had been given the chance."

"I know Bernard and I have really missed you guys," I say. "Just please do me a favor and keep it under your hat while we are at the hospital. Madison is having a really hard time with what happened to Wanda, and I don't want to cause any problems. I just couldn't lie to you about it."

"Of course," he says. "I am just sorry you had to go through all of that alone."

This wasn't the first time that Bernard had apologized to me for something his daughter had done. Over the years, he and the rest of his family routinely told me how sorry they were for the way she treated me. It reminded me of the time I was 11 years old, and Maria laid into me at a family function. After lunch, I walked Bernard and his wife Darcy to the front door.

"David, there is something Darcy and I want to tell you," Bernard says in a serious tone. "We want you to know that we have both tried talking to our daughter about the way she treats you."

"Thanks Bernard," I say, not really knowing what else there was to say, but wanting to make him feel better. "It isn't that bad, really."

"It isn't right David, and we want you to know that our entire family has tried to talk some sense into her over the years," Bernard says with deep regret in his voice. "She refuses to listen to any of us, and we want you to know her actions don't reflect how we feel about you or what we believe in as Christians."

"Thank you Bernard," I say as they both hug me before they leave. "You and your whole family have always been really kind to me, and I will never forget it."

As more people visit, I start to let the ones I am close to know what happened. Everyone is horrified that they weren't told and say the same thing: "We would have prayed for you if we had known." Of course, they have been around the family long enough to know "whose" idea it was to keep it a secret.

A couple of days later, Madison finally decides to remove Wanda's feeding tube. I start to notice that not just Maria and my father are behaving very differently toward me now, but my sisters are, too. While Lisa had never liked me, I always hoped I had a shot at having some type of relationship with Madison.

After all those unreturned phone calls and their no-show at the hospital when I was dying, I am not surprised by their behavior. Whenever they did things that hurt me, I always reminded myself it couldn't have been easy growing up in that house.

I pickup on the vibe and finally realize I am no longer needed or wanted at the hospital.

Everyone is playing a part and the fact is that I no longer have one in this family. Much like a movie script revision, my part in the family has been cut. My character doesn't exist anymore in their minds.

One of the things you learn in Hollywood is to pick up on the signals, especially when it's time to go. No one outright told me to leave; I just sensed from their attitudes and comments that I wasn't welcome. After five days of working from the hospital, I headed back to Los Angeles.

On the flight back to Los Angeles, I thought again about the documentary that I produced about my grandmother in 2009. My clients had flown out from Los Angeles to film her, and it was the first time people in my professional life had met my Texas family. Two days into the shoot, the director and writer asked if they could speak with me privately. We were doing some location shots at a local racetrack.

"David, is there something you have done to your family that we don't know about?" my director asks me point-blank. I immediately know where this is going; I've heard it before from the dozens of people who had met my Texas family over the years.

"Nope," I answer with a shrug. "You would think I'd done something unforgivable, right?"

I always try to deflect negativity with humor, but they weren't going to let it go. The writer chimed in. "David, this isn't right, you have to stick up for yourself. We have never seen you back down like this before!" My clients were used to seeing me fight for them, and they had never seen the "passive" David.

I couldn't very well say that I had done one terrible thing to this family: *I had been born.* So I pointed to my beloved grandmother, the subject of their film, off in the distance.

"You see her?" I asked. "They take really good care of her. That's what matters. They have *their* reasons for how they treat me, I guess, and she doesn't know about them. But as long as they take care of her, I can handle the other stuff."

To this day, I stand by that. My grandmother was *worth* taking the hit.

Two weeks after I flew back to Los Angeles, my grandmother died. I flew back for the funeral. I was prepared to mourn the loss of my favorite person in the world. However, I wasn't prepared for the character assassination and verbal jabs to come.

Yes, funerals are not off limits; this one was one more opportunity for Maria to take her parting shots. She had kindly made the funeral arrangements, and I didn't think about the strategic value of that position.

I should have known better.

There were two funerals, one at the family ranch in Oklahoma at our "family" cemetery, and another in Texas at my grandmother's church. My mother went with me to the one in Oklahoma. Like me, she loved my grandmother very much. While she had heard the stories over the years, she didn't actually get to witness how my father and Maria treated me until that day.

The preacher went on and on about how much my grandmother loved her granddaughters and how they enriched her life. He talked about how each member of the family loved her and was loved by her. I wasn't mentioned. Maria finally got her wish and that day I no longer existed.

My mother knew where the "mistake" had come from, but I was so used to this type of stuff it didn't even phase me.

"I am going to let that preacher know she had a loving grandson too!" she whispered in my ear. I asked her to let it go, but she grabbed the preacher's shoulder and said, "I would like you to meet Wanda's grandson, David. He was also an important part of her life."

The preacher obviously hadn't been told about me, or what he had been told hadn't been positive.

"I'm sorry for your loss son," he said. "Here, take this copy of service." One of Maria's sisters saw what had happened and agreed with what my mother did.

"I am glad you said something," she told my mother. "Because if you didn't, I was going to."

Everyone drove back to Texas on a bus the family had rented, and while I had been offered a seat, I was smart enough to realize the less time I spent around Maria and my father, the better. While my mother flew back to Los Angeles, I got on a plane to Texas. I believe the $350 I spent on the plane ticket to keep me out of the line of fire was the best money I've ever spent.

That's when I ran into problem number two in Texas.

Maria was nice to me the morning of the service, a surprise that immediately put me on guard. She always has an agenda when she is nice to me, and I find out what it is in the car ride to the church.

"Your father and I think it would be best to not tell the family about the motorcycle accident and your time in the hospital," she says, oozing fake sincerity. I had been wondering when she was going to get around to this. Apparently no one in her family had told her that they knew about the accident and my almost dying.

Ours is a family of secrets.

"Sorry, Maria," I say, "but I already told them since all of the reason we were trying to keep this secret were no long valid. Everyone kept asking me how I dropped so much weight."

"You shouldn't have done that!" she snaps.

"Why, Maria?" I ask, knowing the answer already. "Grandma wasn't coming out of that. So why keep it a secret?"

"Because now my family will be angry with me for not telling them what happened!" she snarls at me. "It would be nice if you thought of somebody besides yourself for once!"

So sorry my almost dying interfered with your Mother Teresa act, I think to myself as we drive the rest of the way to church in a pissed off silence.

On the car ride over, I figured I just had to keep my mouth shut a little longer and then I could finally put this whole nightmare behind me. Since I had gotten out of the hospital, I never saw any bright lights come from Maria or my father, just the darkness. Every moment I spent with them was uncomfortable on so many levels.

Just one more day and you're free. I thought to myself. *There is no reason to put up with this crap anymore. They can't hurt grandma now, and it's time to go.*

It was told that Madison would speak since, as Maria put it, "She was the closest to your grandmother." Madison's words were eloquent and heartfelt; she did share a special bond with my grandmother. Again, I really love my sister, and I am very proud of her.

That day at the service for my grandmother was another first for me – the first time I was ever attacked from the pulpit.

While I don't blame Maria's friend Jason for being misled, I do think there is a line that should never be crossed at funerals. I don't care if you heard the guy was the worst person on the planet, you let whoever is at the funeral *grieve.*

Jason was one of Maria's best friends and in my grandmother's Bible study group. He spoke about the loss of Wanda Davis. What he said about my grandmother was true, as he espoused all those qualities that made me love her so much. He then went on to talk about how important my sisters were to my grandmother, which was also very true.

"Her granddaughters Lisa and Madison were the light and happiness in Wanda's life. Madison, a teacher at an impoverished bi-lingual pre-k school, called Wanda every day on her way to work. Lisa, a Harvard graduate and lawyer at a nonprofit organization that defends the rights of those less fortunate, would often check in on Wanda as well during the weekends," Jason says with a fondness in his voice. "Wanda loved her granddaughters more than anything in her life with the possible exception of her son and daughter in law Maria."

"And then," Jason says now switching his voice to a more judgmental tone, "there was her grandson David, who was never around."

Jason pauses for a moment to take a drink of water at the altar. I couldn't believe what I just heard, and the silence is now deafening as the congregation waits for Jason to finish his sip of water. What he just said is still hanging in the air, as I look around the church. All of Maria's family and friends look horrified. Then I turn to Maria, who has a smug grin on her face as Jason glances at her and then continues.

"Wanda leaves this world a better place," Jason continues. "Having touched the lives of so many who were lucky enough to appreciate her and participate in her life. I, along with her granddaughters, son, daughter-in-law and friends will always be grateful that *we* took the *time* to love Wanda the way she loved us."

As Jason leaves the podium, I look around the church again, and Maria's friends and family can't even look me in the eye. The family and most of Wanda's friends know what just happened. They knew the only reason I was ever kept around was the fact my grandmother and I had such a close relationship.

While I know Jason isn't aware of everything that goes on in our family, I am still shocked he would say something like that from the pulpit.

Say I didn't live in Los Angeles, run my own company, and wasn't treated like an unwanted leper in my own family, *even then*, in my opinion, a good Christian still doesn't attack someone who is mourning their loss in a church during the funeral service. However, Maria wanted to establish that there was no pretending: I was no longer wanted.

This is the reason they let me come to the funeral. I think to myself as I replay the last three days in my mind. *Maria wants to take her parting shots and let me know Grandma isn't here to protect me anymore.*

My last day there was the closest I ever came to telling my sisters about our fathers alter ego, "Johnny Russell."

We were at my grandmother's house, which the family had already cleaned out. They left a small pile of stuff on the couch. It consisted of every gift I had ever given my grandmother, along with every picture of me that my grandmother had. They told me I was only allowed to choose any of these items if I wanted something to remember my grandmother by, but nothing more.

While I wasn't interested in the material stuff, I did ask if I could have a couple of copies of the duplicate racing photos she had and was told no. I asked if I could make copies and send the originals back. Again, I was told no. That small pile, all the evidence of my relationship with my grandmother, was the only thing they were allowing me to take.

There was one exception. My father had offered to give me the car my grandmother totaled with the caveat, "I am not sure how much it will cost to get fixed, or even if they can fix it." I told him thank you, but I already had a car. I suggested that, since my sisters had brand new cars, he might consider donating it to charity, although I didn't think a charity would take it.

My main goal in visiting my grandmother's house was to take some time to read letters and other personal documents, things I knew they wouldn't let me take. I started to go through the house and in my own way, quietly and respectfully, wrap up my life with her. I wanted to cherish these last few memories of her in the house.

I had wanted to do this alone but was told that Madison didn't want "anyone" alone in the house. They literally followed me from room to room, as I read letters and tried to say goodbye. I have been trusted with millions of dollars by relative strangers in my business, and yet I wasn't trusted in a house with a 20-year-old bed, a couch and an old TV by my own family. About 40 minutes into this, Madison grew impatient.

"Can you hurry it up a little bit?" she asks, making it clear she wanted

212 THE WORLD LOSES AN ANGEL

me out of my grandmother's house.

"Madison, I am just trying to make some memories of grandma," I reply, and I try to explain what I am doing. "You were lucky enough to have her in your life all the time. I didn't get a chance to spend as much time with her."

"Well, whose fault is that?" She asks indignantly.

At that moment, something in me finally snapped. I know she said it in a moment of grief, and I know she is a good person. I believe she has no clue the type of hell I have been going through. But I'm human too, and I nearly lose it.

"Are you kidding me!!!! You have the gall to tell me to 'hurry up' after everything I have been through to protect you and your perfect life?" I ask angrily, as I am now seeing white I am so pissed. "You have no clue what I have been through to make sure you were always taken care of, you ..."

I glance at my father and Maria. They know exactly where I am headed, and I can tell by the looks on their faces: they're scared I'm going to say it.

I want to.

I want the girls to know the hell I have gone through to make sure they had a good life, always taking the high road with Maria, instead of defending myself, so they wouldn't have to see what their parents were truly capable of.

I never once complained about how I was treated because, even when my grandmother would tearfully apologize for it, I would say, "At least they take good care of the girls, Grandma."

After all I went through to make sure they never found out the truth about Johnny, and they couldn't even be bothered to show up to the hospital. I think to myself as my pain and rage grow. *Not a card, no flowers, not even an email.*

I want to tell Madison the truth about what it feels like to be marginalized and rejected by the family you love, but I stop myself before I say anything and walk out the door.

No one wants to hear the truth in this family, I think to myself angrily as I walk down the street. *They prefer their highly-polished version. To them, I am just the "Bastard Mongrel" who didn't even have the common courtesy to die when I had the chance.*

A couple of blocks from the house, I call Veronica.

"You aren't going to believe this one," I start with no preamble. She has been on call since I got here and texting me constantly. After I catch her up, she starts to calm me down by pointing out the silver lining in the whole thing.

"Just think of it this way; it's the last time they can hurt you," Veronica says calmly. "Come home."

As angry as I was with Madison, in a way I still felt sorry for both her and Lisa. Although they were spared the abuse I went through, I knew it wasn't easy to grow up in that family dynamic. Everything was shrouded in secrecy, deceit, and negativity. Everyone has an agenda. Alliances shift.

Love has to be earned...

Much of my admiration for my grandmother was her unconditional love. But with my father and Maria, everyone had to "perform" and stay inside the lines to be accepted. It was like the family version of "Survivor;" each task you completed brought you closer to winning the game, and the grand prize was being loved.

Most of my life, I didn't even know the game was rigged and for me winning was actually impossible. The roles were assigned like this: Lisa was the Perfect One. The obvious second favorite was Madison. And then there was the mongrel that simply wouldn't die, *me*.

While I was used to my role, I worried about the effect of being second best in the family had on Madison.

This vicious favoritism was something that really bothered Grandma, but she knew she couldn't do anything about it. The only thing she could do was to make sure Madison was aware how much she loved her; just like she did with me. That was the way our grandmother operated, always taking care of the wounded animals or rejected children, the ones that had been cast aside in some ways.

It wasn't just me that saw this favoritism, but a number of family members, people who worked for the family and friends too, all remarked on how appalled they were by the way Maria favored Lisa over Madison.

"Maria doesn't even try to hide it," one employee remarked to me in private. "It must just destroy Madison every time she does it!"

I knew the only bright spot for her was Grandma. Like me, Madison at least had Grandma and her unwavering love to fall back on. This was the main reason I didn't tell the girls about "Johnny Russell" that day and what I had done to protect them from the truth.

I felt a tremendous sadness for Madison because I knew she was aware that the one person who loved her unconditionally was gone. I understood how she felt, even if she didn't realize it at the time. While I didn't like what she said, I realized she had only gotten one, very skewed side of the story and couldn't have known what was really happening.

Or else she knew the reality and didn't want to accept it.

I am the first person to understand not wanting to see your parents in a less than favorable light. Sometimes you don't want to see things for what they are. Everyone was affected by this family dynamic, and I remembered the last time I saw Lisa act out.

I had been sitting in the kitchen minding my own business when Maria walked in and started yelling at me. There was no real cause for the attack, she was just angry and wanted to take it out on someone. Both Lisa and Madison stood there helplessly as their mother berated me for using their washing machine to wash my clothes.

After Maria had stormed out of the room, I tried to make it better for the girls. I didn't want them to feel bad for me since their mother was so transparent in her actions.

"Guys, I am sorry about that one, but there wasn't really anything I could do. The maid told me I could wash my clothes. I didn't think it would be a big deal," I said, but I wanted them to know I was OK. "I do think my visits are helping grandma, and I can handle the blowups. It doesn't really affect me anymore."

"Think of the effect it is having on us!" Lisa said imperiously as if she were talking to a backward child. "What *we* have to go through watching it! You have no idea how it affects *us!*"

For a moment, I just stood there, speechless. I was surprised by Lisa's honesty at that moment. Most people would have at least faked sympathy, but it was a rare moment of candor in our family, when someone actually said what they were really thinking without trying to look good.

Unlike my reaction at my grandmother's house, I was able to mask my disappointment at that moment with Lisa. I didn't say anything or react. Instead, I looked inward and tried to look at her reasoning. I realized that she did have a point, and I continued to remind myself of it over the years, *At least I didn't have to live there full-time.*

It was that thinking that always got me to my default setting of taking the verbal abuse and not defending myself. I was aware that the fallout from my conflicts with their mother upset Madison and Lisa, so I had tried even harder to just walk away instead of standing up for myself.

Now, I realize that I may have made a mistake putting up with decades of abuse. Maria had seemed to sense my reluctance to defend myself and doubled her attacks. She was clearly less concerned about her daughters' feelings than I was, or maybe she realized they didn't care.

Of course, when I finally stood up for myself, I jumped out of the frying-pan and into the fire.

The irony of the situation still resonates. When I walked out of the family, the attacks had stopped, but then I was pulled into an even worse situation with "Johnny Russell." All things being equal, I would have chosen to deal with the emotional shredder Maria any day of the week over witnessing the "Johnny Russell" experience over and over, but I wasn't given that choice.

The next day I got out of Texas as quickly as possible. It was made painfully clear I wasn't welcome there and with Grandma gone, it was best for all if I just disappeared. I figured a lawyer would deal with the will, and the girls had my number if they wanted a relationship. After three years of unreturned phone calls and their no-show at the hospital, it was also painfully clear how my sisters really felt about me.

Instead of facing the reality of the situation and realizing my love for them was one sided, I chalked up their actions to grief.

I was still looking for any excuse to hide from the truth. Occasionally, I thought of how much I went through to keep up the illusion of their perfect world and what I sacrificed. Sadly, I still took pride in the fact that my love for them was so strong that even when they lashed out at me, I kept the secret. Of course, I could never tell them what I had been through, but I hoped they knew how much I loved them.

Not wanting to face the reality of how they felt about me, I was determined to go back to LA and get on with my life.

That turned out to be harder than I thought.

CHAPTER ELEVEN

HEALING

The loss of my grandmother hit me hard, and I threw myself into work as a way to escape. Since the network wanted the film as soon as possible, we were up against a really tough deadline, but everyone did a remarkable job in helping us get the film done on time and on budget. We put a lot of stuff on the screen, for very little money.

Since this was a lower budget film, we edited it in the conference room of my office. I got to see the film in a much rougher state than a producer normally would because Alan and I were friends. I made notes where needed, but Alan and the editor were old pros, so I spent most of my time not getting in the way.

During our last week of editing, Alan asked if I wanted to go to a screening with him.

"Hell, no!" was the first thought that went through my mind.

I had been working 24/7 since I got out of the hospital and I just buried my grandmother. When I wasn't in the office working, I was at home sleeping and trying to regain my strength. However, Alan isn't the type of guy who you can say no to and not feel guilty. Not only is he talented, but he's a really good guy who, as a director, also knows how to get a "yes."

As much as I was dreading going to that screening, I had no way of knowing that it would change my life.

The film was a documentary about the war in Iraq, written by a famous author who had a very specific point of view. It showed the very worst of war and contained images that were haunting, and I found it beyond brutal to watch. After watching it, the last thing I wanted to do was attend the reception.

Because of Alan's insistence that we at least make an appearance, I got a chance to meet the love of my life.

Normally at these types of functions, you talk with someone for five minutes and then move on. It's both a networking and a social gathering, which keeps you constantly moving. I had done more of these than I could count and had it down to a science. I would effortlessly glide from one person to the next without a pause in conversation to stop me or an ego bruised when I moved on.

That all changed the moment I met Sarah. There was a light and energy emanating from her that is difficult to describe. It was unlike anything I had seen up to this point, and we both experienced an instant connection.

"I will never be able to sleep tonight," she said with an emotion in her voice that made me realize she wasn't exaggerating. "I am not going to be able to get those images out of my head."

"Until I met you, I felt guilty about even coming to the reception," I told her, as I started to think about what I saw during The End of Days when I crossed over. "Seeing all that death, pain and destruction…"

"I know," she said as she smiled and put her hand on my shoulder. It was as if she knew what I was feeling and I literally felt a spark of energy between us.

We talked for 45 minutes straight, and as people tried to join our conversation, they quickly realized we were busy. While I don't think we were rude, people very quickly recognized that we were having a private conversation and not just networking.

It was getting late, and I had to work the next day. I had got her number before she had to leave.

"You're not going to do the flaky Hollywood thing and *not* call me, are you?" she asked as she smiled and entered her number into my phone.

"Oh no, *Trust* me when I say, *I am calling you tomorrow!*" I told her, realizing I couldn't wait for tomorrow.

Her smile brightened and then she gave me a mischievous look. "Good! Because I will have to find you and kick your ass if you don't!" And with that, she walked away.

Did I forget to mention Sarah is Argentine/Italian and always tells you exactly what she is thinking? Her directness is one of the many reasons I fell in love with her; I always know exactly where she stands.

When I got home that night, I couldn't get Sarah out of my head. This was very unusual for me, but I felt an instant comfort with her, something I had never felt with another woman. I had come close to loving someone a couple of times before but never before had I felt that instant connection.

Looking back I see that whenever I saw a real chance of a connection, I ran the other direction. The advice my father had given me about women as a child had stuck with me my entire life.

One of the decisions I made in the hospital was to find someone who I could share my life with and trust.

When I got home that night, I decided to take a chance. It was midnight, and I was about to go to sleep. I thought again about the hospital and the promise I made the day I woke up: *I would be honest above all else.*

I texted Sarah – Go to sleep already.

The second I sent it, I immediately experienced all the fear and self-doubt that a lifetime of being rejected by your family brings.

You blew it. I thought to myself. *She is going to think you're weird and isn't going to get the reference to her comment about not being able to sleep because of the images of the film.*

I wrestled with that anxiety for 30 seconds and then I had a sense of calm come over me. I remembered all of the good people in the hospital and on my film production who treated me with both kindness and respect. I realized that while I was exposing myself to potential rejection that there are good people out there and it was possible Sarah was one of them.

If what you feel is real, be 100% honest with her, and you won't blow it. I thought to myself as a sense of calm came over me. *It's okay to risk everything if it feels right.*

I got a text back about two minutes later and with it, our great romance began.

We had lunch the next day, and I kept my promise. I was going to be honest with her in all of my affairs – *but one*. No one needed to know about "Johnny Russell."

That lunch was the most honest I have been with anyone in my life, and I think the same could be said for her too. Of course, the first fifteen minutes, we went through the normal first date stuff and then she started to get more personal.

"What's the longest relationship you have ever had?" Sarah asks a little too casually, and I immediately know what she is really thinking.

Why haven't you ever gotten married? I think to myself. *Good question and it is time to speed this up.*

"You mean why am I not married?" I ask and then quickly answer the question before she can cut me off or deflect. "I could go with some cheesy answer like I never met someone like you before, which is true by the way, but it also has the potential of blowing this and I don't want to risk that."

"Then why haven't you ever gotten married?" she asks quickly, "since you brought it up."

"I never trusted someone enough to fall in love with them," I answer honestly while fighting the self-doubt I feel. "I have been afraid of being that emotionally vulnerable with someone."

"OK, then why the sudden change in your life?" Sarah asks. "And why are you telling me all of this on our first date?"

"I made a promise to myself about five minutes ago," I say confidently, even though I feel like I have just jumped into an icy pool head first. "I wasn't going to lie or in any way try to play games with you. That way if this doesn't work, it won't be because I was anything less than completely genuine and honest. I don't want to lie anymore or play games. Life is just too short."

"So you have been less than honest with other women in the past?" she asks.

"Yes," I say and realize I have nothing to lose as I plow on. "But not in the way you are thinking. I have been brutally honest with most of the women in my life, telling them there is no future in a relationship with me from the very start."

"You know you aren't exactly selling yourself as a boyfriend by telling me all of this," she says jokingly, but I can tell she really likes the fact that I am being so honest, and it encourages me to keep going.

"Let me finish," I say. "Every time I started to get attached to someone I was dating, I ran the other direction. I didn't do this because I wanted to hurt them, but in my mind, I was actually protecting them and myself from eventually getting hurt. At least that is what I thought at the time, but now I realize it was because I was terrified of falling in love and becoming emotionally vulnerable."

"After my divorce, I felt the same way," she says sympathetically.

"You already know about the motorcycle accident and the whole dying thing," I say. "You may be thinking that is why I am being so honest, and that is partially true, but the real reason is that I have never felt this way around another person before. I decided to take a chance and be 100% honest with not only my intentions but also how I really feel. I can promise you that is all you will ever get from me. I will never lie to you."

I looked directly into Sarah's eyes, and I can tell I hit home with what I just said.

"Thank you for being so honest, and I promise to do the same," Sarah says. "This is the first time in years I actually feel like someone is being 100% honest with me. After my divorce and dating a while, I never thought I would find that."

I reach my hand out to hold hers at that moment, and I felt that electric shock again as we touched. From that moment on with Sarah, I realized I had finally come home. I just knew I was done searching for someone to share my life with. There are no real words to accurately describe the feeling that I had finally found my soul mate.

After our first date, we saw each other every day with the exception of eight nights in a period of two and a half years. I firmly believe that God put Sarah in my life to show me there were good people in this world and that it was finally my turn to be loved.

I told anyone who would listen to me that my grandmother had asked God to put Sarah in my life. I think she looked down, saw what had been happening, saw what was about to happen and put Sarah in my life to show me what it was like to be loved.

She was a mirror to my soul and showed me what I had almost become.

Eventually, my time with Sarah made me realize that what my father had raised me to believe was a lie. Women weren't out to get men – that was his projection of the world as he saw it, and a reflection of how *he* treated women.

Unfortunately, if you hear something when you are young from a parent, you don't have the defense mechanisms in place to reject it, if it is negative information. You instinctually imprint on what they are saying as true, and it stays with you. All around us, society perpetuates the idea that your family always has your best interests at heart. Today, I still believe this is true about 99% of the time.

Unfortunately, I had been raised by the 1% in more ways than one.

In my time with Sarah, I started to analyze every core belief I had to make sure it hadn't been infected by my father's thinking, everything from my thoughts on women to the type of father I wanted to be. As I began to interact with her family as a father figure, I started to realize the true depth of my father's issues.

I had grown up with a lot of confusing advice, and I needed to sort through it to find *my truth*. Obviously, I rejected just about everything he had taught me and I knew there was something deeply wrong with him.

Still, he was my father and while he had rejected me almost completely, somewhere deep down I still wanted to believe he cared for me in his own way. At the same time for *my* family's sake, I wanted to make sure my thoughts were that of a good man, not *him*.

Of course, I didn't share any of this with Sarah. I began to think of her and her family as a life raft I had found in a lonely little ocean that had been my life. I was just too afraid of losing them. I knew I wasn't my father's son, so I was no danger to her family.

After a few months of dating and meeting her children, I met the rest of her family. They reminded me a lot of Maria's family, nothing but love and kindness in their hearts. The bonus for me was for the first time in my life; I was actually treated like a valued addition to the family. I was no longer playing the part of the unwanted bastard but judged only on my own actions and merit.

Still, it took me a while to get used to being loved and treated with kindness. There were a number of times I would pull back emotionally for fear of being hurt.

Somehow Sarah sensed I had gone through something traumatic and was very patient with me. Later I found out she thought it was residual trauma from the motorcycle accident. I was kind of like an abused dog looking for table scraps of affection. I was unsure of people's intentions but desperate to connect with them.

I was still very *raw and vulnerable.*

Eventually, I understood that some people could be loving and kind without a hidden agenda, without demanding anything back but love and kindness.

In a weird way, I missed being around Maria's family (not Maria or my father), but Maria's mother, father, brother, sisters, nephews, and cousins who were so kind to me. I imagined introducing them to Sarah and her family. Of course, I knew that was a fantasy and that it was never going to happen.

I told myself I got lucky. God put Sarah and her family in my life to make up for the past. Spending time with Sarah and her family was the most rewarding and important experience in my life, and I will be forever grateful to them.

Ten months after my grandmother's funeral, my father reached out to me. At first, he tried to get me to go on another trip, and I told him no immediately. I slipped by mentioning I was in a serious and committed relationship, and he asked if he could meet her. My opinion of him had changed so much; I really didn't want him anywhere near her or her family.

"There are some things I need to discuss with you in person," he says with a little emotion in his voice. "Things are so much different now that your grandmother has passed."

"I know," I say, and I start to soften a little.

"You know we could just take a small trip," he says and quickly adds. "I could come out and see you in LA, and then we could go to San Francisco. Didn't you like spending time together?"

"Dad, I always like spending time with you. It is the extra people I had the issue with," I say and then add, "spending time with you was the reason I agreed to the trips in the first place!"

"Well, why don't we just do that?" he asks quickly. "There is a lot I want to talk to you about, but not over the phone."

"What do you want to talk with me about?" I ask, but I assume it has something to do with my grandmother's final wishes. It has been ten months since she passed and I hadn't heard anything from anyone about it.

"I can't talk about it over the phone," he says cryptically. "It is something we have to sit down in person and discuss. It will also give me a chance to see how you are doing in life. Are you going to be angry with me for the rest of your life?"

"Dad, I am not angry with you, but things got very intense there for a while," I say. "I am just-"

"I know things got uncomfortable for you," he says interrupting me. "Things were really uncomfortable for me when you checked into Rehab, but I didn't write you off as a son. You know how much it embarrassed and hurt me and your grandmother to see you in that place."

"Dad, I know it couldn't have been easy for you," I say.

"You are not drinking now, are you?" he asks.

"No, of course not," I reply defensively. "I haven't had a drop since our last trip."

"Then why don't you want me to see your new life?" he asks. "What are you trying to hide?"

"I am not trying to hide anything!" I say. "I have a great life now."

"Well, then show me," he says flatly. "What I have to talk with you about has a direct relationship to how well you are doing in your life, but it is something I need to see for myself."

At this point in the conversation, I realized that my father was the executor of my grandmother's will.

Maybe there is some clause in the will that has to have him sign off the final dispensation? I think to myself as he continues to go on and on about how much he has changed. *Maybe grandma's death made him see what he was doing was wrong and he wants to re-establish some type of relationship with me?*

After another 20 minutes of him telling me how much he misses me, how much he has changed and how things are going to be different now that grandma is gone, I relent. I agree to introduce him to Sarah and go with him to San Francisco.

I told him again that I wasn't interested in participating in his life-style choices anymore, and he said, "Relax. We'll be staying at the Dog Hollow Inn." That was a place we stayed at since I was a kid, every time they took the girls on their shopping trips to San Francisco.

Along with finding out what was going on with my inheritance, there was also a part of me that wants my father to see the success I have achieved, both personally and professionally. Deep down, I was hoping my change in social status might finally earn me enough respect that he would treat me like a son and not "David Russell," brother/beard/cleaner.

I wanted to give him another chance to prove I had been wrong about him. Also, I had my eye on a small house I was considering buying with Sarah.

Sarah had her own house, but I was already thinking ahead and dreaming about having our own place together. Maybe if my father saw the love Sarah and I shared, he would see there was such a thing as a healthy man/woman relationship.

Maybe....

I arranged for a dinner reservation at a really nice restaurant in Beverly Hills. A number of deals had finally come through for me, and I wanted to show my father how good my life was going. I was a year sober; my management business was doing really well, and I had just executive produced a ten million dollar film that had just wrapped in New York, starring three Academy Award nominees.

He asked me to come to his hotel about five hours early, and I figured he wanted to go over the paperwork regarding my grandmother's estate.

I was wrong.

When I arrived at his hotel, he told me he wanted to visit a "friend" of his in Ventura about an hour and a half away. One look in his eyes, and I knew he was on another "trip." He was acting a little twitchy, and I began to wonder what he was on. I also started worrying about dinner. I knew I couldn't cancel without telling Sarah everything, and the fact is that it took some work to get this dinner reservation.

I start to race through my options in my mind. Option one is to say, "Screw you, I'm done!" but I know this is not a smart move right now. As much as I want to do exactly that, he is the executor of my grandmother's estate. Nothing would make him happier than to have an excuse to screw me out of my inheritance.

Pissing "Johnny" off, by not conforming to his every demand has consequences, and I have seen them first hand. Also, I have already been shown the door by the family. I am vulnerable, and he knows it. Option number two is to drive him out there and hope I get *happy* "Johnny" back that way, the only person who suffers is me, and it's only one afternoon.

"If you want, I can drop you off somewhere," I say, reluctantly. "But I am *not* going inside."

"Sure, no problem! And we can be back in plenty of time for dinner!" he replies happily.

On the way to Ventura, I catch a break and start negotiating a deal for one of my clients on a film for Marvel. I thank God for the distraction. It's something that I had been working on for a little bit and gives me an excuse to not talk to "Johnny."

I start to feel all of the old emotions of being on another trip with "Johnny." But as I am negotiating the deal, I realize I am feeling something new this time. The guilt and shame of being "Johnny's" beard/brother/cleaner remains, however, I am now experiencing a new feeling.

Anger.

For the first time since this whole thing began, I start thinking about myself and what "Johnny's" behavior has done to me. I also start to wonder why I had never felt angry before?

There is something different in my life and about me. *Sarah.*

When we get to Ventura, he asks me to drop him off at one of those low-rent massage parlors that line the boulevard. He asks me to stay close, and I use the time to finish the deal, trying not to think of what he is doing. He makes a half-hearted attempt to pay for a massage for me, "Just a regular one," he says, but I decline the offer.

I drive down the street, park the car in front of a store that sells every bottled soda you can imagine and start closing the deal. Two hours go by and finally, I get the call to pick him up. When he gets in the car, my nose is assaulted by whatever perfume the prostitute was wearing. I am not a delicate man, but even I can't take the smell, and I quickly roll down the windows. "You're going to have to take another shower before dinner," I tell him.

He doesn't get it. "I took one there!" he protests.

"Well, whatever you showered in smells like a French whorehouse, and you can't go to dinner with Sarah smelling like that!" he sees I am pissed and lets it go.

I am about two seconds away from saying the hell with this and just letting the lawyers handle the estate. I concentrate on just getting through the dinner and remembering that once this final business is settled, I don't have to have him in my life anymore.

He is never going to change. I think to myself. *And I don't want him infecting my new life.*

I didn't know quite what to expect when it came to the one-third of my grandmother's estate she had promised me. I knew it would be a nice sum of money that could help Sarah and me find a house together, and maybe I could invest the rest of it for retirement. The truth is, I never really thought about it except as a nice future boost, a kind of financial cushion that would allow me to take time off if I needed it, or start a new business, or even fund a charity in my grandmother's name. These were all just vague plans I had, knowing what my grandmother had promised.

It's these plans that help me keep my temper in check while we drive back to his hotel. He must sense my anger because he tries to get me to feel sorry for him.

"Things are going to be different with your grandmother gone," he says and I assume he means how much the family will feel the loss of her.

"There was no one like her," I say sincerely. I think of my grandmother, and I thank God she never found out about this side of my father.

No matter what happens now, at least grandma never met Johnny Russell. I think to myself. *It would have killed her, hell it almost killed me...*

My father starts to mention our trips together, and what fun "we" had, and before he can suggest that we try again, I steer the conversation around to how much he's going to like Sarah. I focus on trying to keep the conversation away from anything, but how wonderful Sarah is and how much she has changed my life for the better. Unfortunately, this takes my mind off my driving, and I take the wrong exit, and we get lost. My father immediately becomes scared and agitated.

"Relax," I tell him, not really understanding why he's so frightened. "I think I took a wrong turn, and I just want to figure out how to get back on the right road."

Later it occurs to me that "Johnny" was worried that I had finally had enough of him and was going to take him on the side of the road and kick the crap out of him. Of course, this doesn't happen, and we drive the rest of the way back to the hotel in silence.

After getting out of the shower at his hotel, my father tells me that he is looking forward to going to San Francisco and spending some quality time together. I just smile at him, but my stomach is twisting in knots at the thought of spending any more time alone with him.

At this point, I'm trying to keep myself calm.

He seems normal now, but I have seen too many versions of him to be confident that one of his other personas doesn't rear its ugly head. I tell myself that it's just dinner and then back to his hotel. We don't have to pretend much; I have already told Sarah that I have a strained relationship with him. I just didn't give her the horrifying details. Still, I can't shake the feeling that this is a bad move.

Luckily the dinner goes off without a hitch. Everything is going great, and Sarah suggests we have dessert back at her place.

"That sounds like a great idea!" my father quickly replies. However, I am the opposite of happy. My blood pressure has jacked up 100 points since hearing the suggestion, but saying anything without saying *everything* simply won't work. Since we took separate cars, my father and I are the first to arrive at Sarah's house.

"Nice place," my father says as he looks the front of the house up and down. "Too bad you will never be able to afford to keep her in it."

Are you trying to piss me off? I think to myself. *What is wrong with you?*

That is when I see "Johnny" smirking back at me, and I realize I don't want this to escalate at Sarah's house and try to diffuse the situation.

"Actually, I am doing pretty well at the moment, but thanks for the vote of confidence," I say confidently as I unlock the front door.

We walk into the house, and Sarah gives him a tour a couple of minutes later. Dessert and coffee take about 20 minutes, but I still can't hide the tension I feel as a result of my father being in Sarah's house. I get him out of there as quickly as possible and drop him back off at his hotel.

That night, I had an epic "night terror."

Sarah is beginning to realize the "night terrors" have nothing to do with the motorcycle accident. Apparently, I leapt out of bed that night screaming, "NO!!!" at the top of my lungs. Sarah had to scream my name to snap me out of it. When I came to, I was panting, standing in a boxer's position, fists up, ready to fight.

"Please don't go. Just tell him you're sick," she says that morning as I pack my bags for the trip.

"Relax," I say with a confidence I don't feel. "It is just a couple of days, and we need to talk about my grandmother's final wishes anyway."

"I know he is your father, and you've said you have had a difficult relationship with him," Sarah says with her voice full of love and concern, "but I have to tell you that I have a really bad feeling about him. It's like ..." she searches for the words. "It's like he's *a reptile*, the way he looks at you!"

I laugh it off and tell her she is imagining things. But it sticks with me, and I know she is right.

As soon as my father and I get off the plane, he suggests we get a massage. I immediately say, "No!" But he assures me it's a legitimate place and a massage might help with the cold I have developed. Being around "Johnny" has literally made me sick. I check out the massage parlor myself this time, and it looks legit, still it takes me a while to relax while getting a normal massage.

After the massage, he decides he wants to visit another massage parlor where a "friend" of his works. I tell him I am not feeling well and want to go back to my room. He heads toward the massage parlor without a word, and I realize we are only three blocks from the hotel. We have stayed here since I was a kid, and I begin to ask myself, "*How long has this been going on?*"

When I get back to the room, I see Sarah has emailed me a couple of times. Since she picked up on my anxiety being around my father, she has been emailing and texting me nonstop since we got here. I call her ten minutes later and tell her I am fine, but no one can really hide from the person they love most.

"Why don't you just come home early?" she pleads with me. "I can book a ticket for you now, all you have to do is get in a cab. I have the reservation section up on my computer now."

I love her so much at that moment; no one has ever even tried to rescue me that way before.

Still, I can't leave. I figure he is waiting until the end of the trip to get into the details of the estate. I can hold out one more day. Sarah doesn't know about "Johnny" at this point and I wished I had told her everything. As much as I didn't like the thought of him infecting my new life with her, I knew she deserved to know the truth.

When I finally did tell her months later, she couldn't understand why I'd allowed him to come to her house. She looked at me with pity in her eyes, as I told her how I was hoping my worst fears about my father weren't true. I had hoped my grandmother's passing had made him realize the errors of his ways. That, coupled with all of my success, would hopefully bring my old father back and I would finally earn his love and respect.

I apologized to her then as I do now.

In what would be the last night I spend out with "Johnny," we go out to eat and catch a movie. At dinner, the woman at the table next to us got very drunk and started flirting with me. She was with some male coworker friends, and I could tell "Johnny" was hoping I would go for her and risk ruining what I had with Sarah. He tried to encourage me to take the next step with the woman, but I told him I wasn't interested.

That night, I think "Johnny" realized I was never going to be his beard again. That I would never approve of his behavior. That I would never, *ever* follow in his sordid footsteps. As we walked back to the hotel, he started asking me questions.

"You think you are going to marry Sarah?" he asks me, when we are about three blocks from the motel.

"If I am lucky, and she says yes," I say, knowing where this is going: the family line. We stop walking for a moment as he buys a single rose from a florist.

"She obviously can't have any more kids, have you thought of that?" he asks me looking me directly in the eyes now.

"Yes," I say staring right back at him. "But she already has 3 kids, and they have allowed me to become a part of the family. I'm really lucky that I get to share in their lives now."

"But they won't be yours!" he says and I can see the anger and disappointment in his eyes. Before I can say anything, he turns away from me and heads for the massage parlor with a rose in his hand.

That trip we never discussed my grandmother's estate. He held it as bait until the very end, and the one time I brought it up, he claimed he wanted to talk about it later. I decided to wait another month until I got my ducks in a row and the truth is, I wasn't hurting for money at the time. I figured I would ask him one more time.

I should have known that, like everything else with my father, it could never be easy or fair.

As I rode the tram to my gate, I did my post-trip damage assessment. Most of the damage was contained to my relationship with Sarah: I felt guilty for introducing her to my father. I had hoped he had changed, but the fact is that he never failed to disappoint me, as a man and as a father. This trip was no exception. And I realized that this wasn't an aberration. He'd admitted as much in San Francisco when he slipped and described one of the massage parlors as a place he has been going to *"for years."*

I knew at that moment, in no uncertain terms, that my father had no use for me as a person or a son. We would never have the relationship I'd hoped for. It was clear now that we would never have *any* kind of decent relationship. I was tired of being hurt and rejected and disappointed; I had found a new, happier path, and that new happiness had prepared me to let go of fantasies that would never come to pass. So I did. I let go.

I didn't know releasing him in that way would peel back the final layers and reveal the much more vicious, amoral creature beneath. I was about to face the greatest adversary of my life.

CHAPTER TWELVE

THE UGLY TRUTH

I just wanted to be free of all of it. The lies, family secrets, low rent brothels, and horrifying behavior.

After his trip to Los Angeles and San Francisco, I realized there was no more denying "who" my father was at his core and that I could no longer believe *anything* he told me. I saw now that all of my father's actions pointed to the fact he was a parasite that only knew how to use people for his own gain and then throw them away.

Looking back, I can see it started shortly after I was born.

Once my mother put my father through medical school, he divorced her as soon he finished his residency. Without her, he never would have gotten into that medical school. She had been working for the head of admissions at the time and she convinced her boss to re-write the admission policy for my father; his grades didn't cut it for their admissions standards.

Once he finished medical school, he had immediately divorced her.

While I had heard part of that story when I was young, I discovered more while I was writing this book. Apparently he gave her an ultimatum, he told my mother that he was willing to stay married to her, but wanted to live at the hospital where he was dating several nurses. He still wanted to look the part of a family man, but not be burdened with actually having to be a faithful husband and father.

It turns out he has always just been looking for a "girlfriend."

My father waited until my mother had put him through school, had a small child and no real choices, before announcing his true intentions. With her in this weakened position, he stood the best chance of getting what he wanted. He gave no regard to the fact my mother had worked to support him all of those years, like the end of the trip in Cancun with Patricia, he was done with her.

In his mind, I am sure he thought he had been magnanimous, after all, he had offered to stay married to her, just not faithfully. I think he felt he was no longer obligated to think of anyone but himself, now that he reached his goal of becoming a doctor.

I believe it was this early sense of entitlement and the small group of people who continue to enable him that most likely played a role in creating the "Johnny Russell" of today. In the beginning, we all started out with the best of intentions; we weren't enabling him, but trying to help him.

They say the pathway to hell is often paved with good intentions, and I was about to find out how true this is.

Even though I *knew* I had been used by my father, somewhere deep inside of me I hoped my father at least thought of me as his son. In my mind, all of the years we had spent together had to count for something!

I was wrong.

Twelve months after my grandmother passed, I still hadn't heard anything about her last wishes. Realizing my father was going to avoid dealing with this as long as possible, I finally put a call into him. I was doing my taxes, and I needed to know what to tell my accountant. There was a certain glee in his voice as he told me what had happened.

"It all goes to me," he told me as I listened, stunned. "And if there is anything left when I die, it will go to you and your sisters."

My grandmother had never lied to me in my life, and she had told my sisters what she had told me as well. Somehow, my father had convinced my grandmother to give him authority over the trust she had set up for all three grandchildren.

"I don't understand. This goes against everything grandma told us," I say, so stunned I can barely utter the words. "Was Grandma lying to us when she told us everything was to be split a third to each of us when she passed?"

"No, she wasn't lying. But this is the way it is, and there's nothing you can do. I've been planning this since the custody case," he says with smug satisfaction.

Since the San Francisco trip I knew that my father was not only "Johnny Russell," but *that was all he was*. That was the man he had been my entire life. Still, I had wondered why he kept up the show of loving me, and now I was getting my answer.

"I have total control of all of the money your grandmother left," he says with an unmistakable joy in his voice. "When I die it, *if* there is anything left, it will be split equally between you, Lisa and Madison. But they get theirs immediately," he adds and then continues with venom in his voice. "*You* will get yours when you're 60 and *only* in monthly installments. When you die, the *rest* of it goes to the girls."

It takes me a moment to process all of this as I sit in my car stunned.

I'm thinking about the house I was dreaming about and my new life with Sarah. I am thinking about my sweet grandmother and how her last wishes are being violated by her own son. Not only is he prostituting her last wishes, but he is treating my sisters and I exactly the way he did Cindy in Vegas.

He is getting off on this!

"This goes against everything Grandma wanted," I finally manage to say. "You know I am not going to sit still while you do this. This is just wrong on every level!"

"It doesn't matter now," he says, "because I have control of it and even if you sue me, you won't get anything. I already hired the best lawyers money can buy."

Deep, deep down I was worried something like this might happen to me, but now he is doing it to my sisters as well. He knows this will hurt me and continues to push the knife deeper as he says, "Also, I want you to know I am leaving you nothing of what I have put together over the last 40 years."

"Why are you doing this?" I ask again, and I am reeling at this point. "I have only ever put the family first! I've been a loyal son even when it cost me everything!"

"Because," he says simply. "I planned it this way. I'm doing what I think is best for you. Also, some of the money that was supposed to be left to you has been commingled with our community property. Maria has gone after it, and we are trying to work that out with the lawyers now."

After a little more back and forth in which nothing is explained, he hangs up.

It takes me some time to sort out the truth. My father has control of our inheritance, but won't give it to me or my sisters, claiming to be looking out for us. That's when I started to wonder what he is *really* going to do with the money. He has some very expensive habits, and I am not sure if my sisters know about them.

At that moment, there was no longer a doubt in my mind that he saw not just *me, but my sisters* as "expendable" as well. Why else would he treat us this way?

I tried to work it out with him and made several more calls. I put on my manager hat and tried to remove any and all the emotion out of the conversation, as I untangle the financial facts from fiction. It did not go well. He soon started behaving irrationally, for example, bringing up my *cholesterol* in the middle of my repeating what he had done.

He soon realized he didn't have to pretend to care about me anymore and would frequently just hang up the phone.

I was persistent as I put the pieces together. My father had used my alcoholism against me, convincing my Grandma to leave the money to him so that he could distribute it. He used everything I ever told him in confidence against me to keep the inheritance for himself. What I couldn't understand, and still don't, is how he convinced her to leave the girls' inheritance to him as well?

I don't blame my grandmother. She was a very simple and kind woman. She only wanted the best for me, and I know she had never met "Johnny," or even imagined that such a creature existed. It wouldn't have been too hard to buy the concerned doctor/father bit. He had used it on countless women, and even I had wanted to believe it until I met "Johnny." I knew that if my grandmother had any clue who my father really was, she would never have given him control over the inheritance she wanted to leave my sisters and myself.

I think he really enjoyed those initial calls, watching me struggle to accept who he really was. My life with him had been a lie, not just the one with "Johnny" but all of it, the girls, his wife and him as my father. He had played the long game to get the money, the ranch, the oil wells and he had won.

Eventually, "Johnny" stopped taking my calls, and I tried one last ditch effort.

I went to our family Pastor and asked him for guidance through this. I admitted that I was angered by what my father had done, but it was much deeper than just a money issue. I could take the hit financially, and I knew eventually I would earn my own dream house and a comfortable retirement. But he had kept my sisters' inheritance as well, and they didn't know about "Johnny Russell."

They didn't know that our father wasn't to be trusted.

I also contacted the Pastor because I was finally ready to atone for what I'd done and make things right with God. I flew out to Texas and met with our pastor in his church office; I got down on my knees and begged God for forgiveness. We prayed together for mercy, and we prayed for the family to heal.

I could write an entire book on how much Pastor Landon helped me, but out of respect for him and his privacy, I am only paraphrasing the truly crucial advice he gave me. He is a good man who helped me greatly. The reason I even included him in this book at all is the fact that I benefited from his spiritual advice and it is something I want to share with others.

I want to share Pastor Landon's wisdom with others as he is pure of heart and intention. He only wanted to help heal my family through prayer and counseling.

After praying with Pastor Landon, I felt the first real relief since this whole thing started. Because of his guidance, I still pray every morning before work, and I thank God for the blessings in my life, my family, my friends and the gifts I have been given. I will always have gratitude in my heart for him.

Pastor Landon and Sarah were the two biggest blessings in my life at that time, and they enabled me to survive my father's betrayal. He wasn't technically my Pastor but the family Pastor, and although he had never heard of something like this, he prayed to help heal my soul.

The "night terrors" had gotten consistently worse after my father had revealed his true intentions and the family went radio silent at that point. I had tried to reach out to Lisa and Madison when I was in town, but they were both too busy to see me.

Sadly all of my fears of family abandonment were becoming a reality as well.

I really wish my grandmother hadn't repeated to me (and others) her wishes; it would have saved me a huge headache and heartache. I felt guilty that my silence had enabled my father to do this to not only me but my sisters as well.

Had my grandmother never told me her intentions, I would have simply mourned the loss of her and never given a thought of what she did with the money. But she told everyone within earshot of her plans, every time she saw us. My father went so far as to confirm it at a Thanksgiving lunch.

"Think of how nice your grandchildren's lives will be when they inherit the money you're making on Laughlin Manor," my father said grandly referring to the real estate venture my grandmother had backed. It made millions.

The burden to make things right lay solely on my shoulders as a man, and I knew it. Just like that, another brick had been added to my backpack. The night terrors came back with a vengeance, and Sarah helped me through them the best she could.

In one of the six and a half hours of conversations my father and I had, he told me he deserved to get Laughlin Manor when my grandmother passed because, "I spent all of that money fixing up the house she lived in. I deserve it," he said self-righteously. To be fair, he did fix up the place, but that was because he owned it and my grandmother paid him rent.

Also, it wasn't worth millions.

In a twisted way, I think he enjoyed turning one of the most honest people I have ever known into an unintentional liar. He really seemed to get off on perverting anything that was good or pure. He seemed to enjoy taunting me on the phone during our conversations.

Maybe he was trying to goad me into a relapse? I wondered as he continued to threaten and taunt me over the phone. *He knows I am happy with Sarah and will never enable him while I am sober.*

After our initial meeting, the Pastor told me that he didn't think there was a lot he could do, given the circumstances. He promised to pray for the family and me, but thought I stood a good chance in losing my family if I continued to pursue it; he was willing to try a spiritual intervention of sorts, but he wanted me to know the risks.

Would my father agree to spiritual counseling? I wondered. *Was he even capable of sincere contrition?*

Knowing the family, and confident I had already tried everything, I went over the options again and again. I thought about the inheritance, and what I'd planned to do with it. I also thought about what the truth would do to my sisters.

I made a small donation to the church and decided to give my father a year to think about what he had done. Because I still considered them family, even after all this – I just couldn't do it; I couldn't tell them about "Johnny Russell." I had some small hope that my father would eventually see the line he crossed.

Seven months later, I got an invitation to Madison's wedding. I really wanted to go, and hoped I might work some things out with my father. The night terrors continued to plague me, but I thought of them as my penance for my part in enabling "Johnny," with my silence. Once Madison announced her marriage, I realized I had an obligation as her brother to try and get my father to at least give the girls their inheritance.

While I was comfortable financially, my sister Madison is a school teacher, and she was living on a school teacher's salary. I wanted my father to honor my grandmother's wishes so that she could start her life off more comfortably.

Also, I didn't want to go to the wedding pretending everything was "fine," and I was determined to get him to see that he had a serious problem and needed help. I was done being complicit and enabling my father to hurt the rest of the family.

As you might imagine, the calls didn't go well.

I tried to start the conversation calmly, avoiding any mention of money for me, and told him I wanted to go to my sister's wedding, but there were some things we need to discuss. My main concern was the fact my sister was starting a new life and deserved to have the money she was promised by grandma to do it. I also told him I felt an obligation as her brother to make sure this happened.

He saw my genuine concern for her as a threat and responded in kind.

"The money in the will is left to me, and I can do what I want to with it," he says angrily. "You will never end up seeing anything if you keep pushing this!"

"That's fine," I say calmly. The truth is I have accepted that. It stopped being about money a long time ago.

"If you go ahead and take this to court or something like that," he goes on, "you'll just be squandering the percentage of the money that you *might* get – if I see fit!"

He is obviously trying to start a fight. "Ok, Todd, first of all – "

"You know who uses the word Todd for his father?" he interrupts. "A 13 or 14-year-old boy."

"No, Todd is basically the person I am talking to because my biological father would never have involved me in the things you have. If you want to discuss *that*, great. *That's* the thing I am upset about," I say after listening to him threaten me for ten minutes and stick to the point of my call.

"I am on the phone with you because your actions almost cost me my life, and because I think you have a problem with sexual addiction," I say after he attacks my motives yet again.

"Your mother and I never wanted you to get a motorcycle," he says weakly, completely ignoring what I just said. "I don't want to talk to you anymore about this. You know I do not do well with blackmail."

"How am I trying to blackmail you?" I ask him.

He struggles a half second with that one. "You're making me angry," he says lamely. "You're threatening to go to court."

Are we even having the same conversation?

"I haven't threatened to go to court!" I say. Again I tell him that I'm not threatening anything, I just want to talk about some issues in a very calm manner. He tries to deflect again and then hangs up before I can reply.

I don't know what I was hoping for. Regret? Acknowledgement? *Something*?

Next, I tried to talk with Maria. I *really* wanted to see Madison get married.

I tried to be as gentle as possible on the call. I told her I wasn't comfortable with going to the wedding without telling her exactly why I was so angry with my father. However, I knew the second I mentioned specifics I would be kicked out of the family for good this time, and I was afraid she would hang up. I tried to be as tactful and delicate as possible and told her I wanted to talk about a "serious" issue my father had that I was worried about.

"Why don't you walk away until January – after my birthday, after Madison's wedding and after our trip?" she asks me calmly as she continues to deflect by placating me with, "then whatever...You can do whatever it is you want to do, but it doesn't sound like it's going to help anybody in the next three weeks."

"I know this is coming from left field for you, and I am trying to do the right thing here, but this had been killing me for seven months," I say, but I can tell she doesn't care. "And I know you are thinking like yeah, sure David, whatever...but I have always put Lisa and Madison first my entire life, and I have swallowed a lot because of it."

"David," she says trying to interrupt me.

"I am trying to tell you this as a courtesy, so we can get the right people involved," I continue, and she interrupts me again.

"David, that is all bullshit, and you know it. Please," she says. "You didn't even know their addresses, their emails, how to spell their names. You have never known. So don't tell me you put them first."

"I have never known?" I ask, not understanding and then it hits me.

She is trying to re-write history again. I think to myself as she continues her rant. *The worse she makes me look, the better her chances of them getting away with this.*

"Don't tell me you care about them so much because you have never displayed-," she continues, but I finally interrupt her.

"Maria, do you know that since you and I stopped talking, I have called them once every three weeks for four years and didn't get a response?" I ask her interrupting her because I just can't take it anymore.

"No," she says after a moment of silence.

"I left a message each time saying, 'I love you and please give me a call back if you have the time,' and I never got a call back from them," I say.

"So there is not a relationship there, is what you are telling me? And it is not your fault?"

"No, I am just saying that as soon as we stopped talking-"

"You are always not talking to someone," Maria says defensively. "What does that say?"

"That maybe there is something to work on regarding the relationship?" I answer but start to realize that she is trying to sidetrack me from talking about my father's issues. As much as I have tried to avoid a fight, she is trying to push my buttons.

She is doing everything she can to avoid this, and I am falling into the same trap I always do with her, I think to myself as she tells me she doesn't have time to talk about this, and she has to start packing for her big trip to Europe.

Any doubt I had about Maria not knowing what is going on are erased during this conversation. It isn't what she says, but areas she tries to avoid on the call. I give it one last ditch effort and plead with her.

"I want to go to Madison's wedding," I explain, "but I'm not sure I can be around Todd after what he has done."

"Well then, you can't come if you're not going to be able to control yourself!" she snarls.

So those are my choices: play along or stay away. I appreciate that she is trying to protect Madison's special day, but she is doing exactly what I feared she would do. She is threatening to isolate me from the family unless I play along.

"I'm trying to handle this the right way," I admit.

I wait for some response or question. Maybe something like, *"Handle what the right way?"* But she says nothing, no response, no questions, just silence on the other end of the line.

She has really known all of this time. I think to myself.

"You really don't want to know anything do you?" I ask her point blank in one last attempt to get it out there.

"Not right now, David. First of all, there is nothing I can do about it," she says in a less than pleasant tone. "And I don't need a wedge driven between him and me."

She goes on to say that she can't change him...that he makes his own decisions... *that she loves him no matter what.*

I took one more shot at reaching my father. Instead of talking about his sexual addiction or whatever it was, I tried to convince him I was just trying to look out for my sisters. I simply wanted proof that my sisters had received their share of grandmother's inheritance, as promised.

After that, I insinuated I would go away if he would simply do right by my sisters. He tries once again to deflect my concern and make it about me wanting the money. I answer that question immediately.

"Listen," I finally say, "I have money. Remember the deal I closed when I drove you to the whorehouse in Ventura? I made twenty grand on that call alone."

"Great," he replies. Not a word about proving my sister's inheritances and the fulfillment of at least two-thirds of my grandmother's wishes. The amount has, by now, shrunk to about a third of what he originally mentioned.

Do I believe anything he tells me at this point? I wonder as he continues to tell me the money is now his, and he can do *anything* he wants with it. After threatening me some more, he hangs up.

There was a part of me that wanted to go the wedding and confront my father.

I wanted to tell everyone, everything and expose "Johnny" to the rest of the family. I considered flying in Cindy from Vegas as my "date;" it would have been worth it to see the look on my father's face. But I wasn't willing to ruin Madison's day. I wasn't about to contaminate a happy family occasion forever with evidence of my father's sad, sick double life.

I knew I wasn't like "Johnny," and I wanted to do everything I could to avoid hurting my family while still protecting their interests.

After one more conversation with Maria, trying to get her to at least talk about it, I simply let it go. I stopped reaching out to that side of the family. I couldn't be a part of the happy normal family lie anymore, and I knew no one was interested in hearing the truth. They stopped calling me as well. I was too dangerous because what I knew threatened to destabilize their carefully crafted public lives and reputations.

Along with Pastor Landon, Sarah insisted I see a psychologist specializing in nightmares that a friend had suggested to her. At first, I resisted seeing someone, but as the months wore on the night terrors, became more intense. One night I woke up, and Sarah was screaming at me to wake up.

"What's wrong?" I ask Sarah, as I realize I am standing on top of the wooden trunk at the end of our bed. "How did I get here?"

"David, you had another night terror," Sarah tells me gently. "Are you okay?"

"I am so sorry, Sarah," I say quietly as I step down from the trunk. "I thought the floor was on fire."

"Just come back to bed, honey," she says tiredly, and I realize she is covering how scared she is. "We can talk about it tomorrow."

"Give me the number of the psychologist you were telling me about," I say as I pull the covers over me. "I will set up a meeting with him this week."

"Thank you," Sarah says quickly, and I can hear the relief in her voice.

Two days later, I walked into Dr. Daniels office and told him everything. A seventy-year-old man of Eastern European descent, he said very little but had an extremely impressive resume. With his snow-white beard, he looked more like Santa Claus than a therapist, but he was the opposite of "Jolly."

He always seemed to be studying me.

I spent the next six weeks catching him up on everything I had gone through with my family and my introduction to my father's alter ego "Johnny Russell." At the end of our sixth session, I realized he had said about fifty words since I first walked into his office.

"I am not trying to be a jerk or anything, but are you ever going to say anything other than, 'How did that make you feel?' or 'Go on' in these sessions?" I ask when I realize I only have five minutes left in this session.

Dr. Daniels smiles and asks, "David, why did you become a manager?"

"You are kidding, right?" I respond sarcastically.

"Humor me," he says and after a moment, I realize he is serious.

"I love film, television and working with artists," I say after giving it a moment of thought.

"I think it is more than that, David," Dr. Daniels says in a cryptic tone that makes me realize I am about to get a lecture. "Remember when I asked you what a manager does in our first session?"

"I guess," I say.

Dr. Daniels starts to flip through the pages on his legal yellow legal pad and find what he is looking for and says, "You told me without hesitation, 'A manager protects a clients interest, builds their careers and nurtures their creative identity until they become their own brand.' What role in a family unit does that remind you of?"

"A father," I say after a moment.

"Exactly," he says. "You treat your clients like your children, not only because you don't have any of your own, but also it gives you an opportunity to behave in a way that reflects how you think a father should act and not the way your father treats you."

"I don't see what any of this had to do with my night terrors," I say a little defensively.

"For the last six weeks, I have listened to you tell me your story," Dr. Daniels continues as he looks me directly in the eyes. "Every time I asked you how the abuse felt, you made a joke or deflected, and sometimes even tried to defend their actions."

"I am not saying what they have done is-," I say, but he puts up his hand, and I stop.

"Please allow me to finish," Dr. Daniels says as he puts his hand down. "In your entire career as a manager, have you ever treated a client the way your father and his wife have treated you?"

"I don't know if you can really apply what I do for a living to a family situation," I say weakly as the timer goes off.

"Think about it and we can discuss it next week," Dr. Daniels says calmly, as I get up from the sofa and leave the office.

At first, I thought Dr. Daniels was just reacting to my question and hadn't really thought things through. As I got into my car, and I began to think about what he just said as I started the car.

I have always taken pride in the fact that I put my client's interests first. I thought as I drove home. *I treat them the way I would want to be treated if the roles were reversed.*

The cold hard truth was Dr. Daniels was right.

In a million years, I would never treat my clients the way my father and Maria treated me over the years. I finally realized sitting at a stop light. *Because I value my clients, and I could never treat them like they were expendable...*

CHAPTER THIRTEEN

THE GOOD SON

My father's favorite thing to say to me when I was a boy was, "Let's go pick up some girls, David." Back then, my father got to see me during the summers, and he made good use of the time. By age 6, I could get a girl's number and introduce them to my father in five minutes flat.

I always approached them alone, ensuring they wouldn't leave the poor little "lost" boy before my father came to the rescue. He would admonish me for "sneaking away," and then make his move on whichever woman we "picked up."

As we backpacked all over the world, he would often leave me with strangers while he hooked up with whichever girl "we" had picked up. I used to look back on those times fondly, "bonding" as father and son. I didn't realize it at the time, but I had joined his long list of enablers before I lost all of my baby teeth.

When I was nine, Maria got a chance to meet "Johnny Russell," and in a way, I feel sorry for her. They had been going out for about a year at that point, and she was my best friend. I would learn that like Patricia, she thought having me on her side would strengthen her case in winning over my father.

That summer my father and I were skinny dipping with a few of his nurses at his house. I politely took their bras and panties from them, as I folded them up neatly, putting them on the table next to the pool. Even back then, I unknowingly represented safety to his conquests.

Maria came home early that day and marched off indignantly when she caught us.

My father asked me to call her on the phone and beg for forgiveness on his behalf. Since they hadn't married yet, Maria had bent over backward to show me I could trust her and that she was my friend. I was hoping that my "friend" would understand that my father and I didn't mean to hurt her feelings.

On that phone call, I got the first glimpse of the "real" Maria.

"You obviously were enjoying yourself, I saw you trying to hide your erection behind the Jacuzzi Jet!" Maria snarled at me on the phone.

She was right, I was trying to hide it since I was nine, I didn't really know what it had meant to have one. Eventually, Maria forgave my father, and they got married. Once that happened, I got a chance to see a lot more of the "real" Maria, and it was the opposite of a pleasant experience.

Whether Maria thought she could change him or whether she thought the money and social station she would achieve was worth the risk is something I will never know. I will also never know if she was offered a similar deal to the one my mother was offered, but like me, she took the gradual path towards darkness many decades ago.

At least I was just lucky enough to get off of it in time to save my soul.

As I recount this story from my childhood for Dr. Daniels, I see him shake his head and set down his yellow legal pad on the end table next to his chair. It has been four months of seeing him now and after the initial question about why I became a manager, we have fallen back into the routine of me doing all the talking while he listens.

"David, do you think you will ever get your family to love you?" Dr. Daniels asks.

"Have you been listening to a word I have said?" I ask.

"What I am asking is, do you really think there is anything you can do to change your father and Maria's feelings toward you?" Dr. Daniels asks in a calm and rational tone that bothers me a little.

"Well, it's pretty obvious how they feel about me," I say. "You proved that with the whole client question."

"Yes, but you continue to try and earn their love," he says.

"Where are you getting that from?" I ask defensively. "I am not a total idiot. They have made it perfectly clear that they wished I was never born. I haven't said anything in any of our sessions to indicate I don't see that!"

"Have you said, 'I still want my family to love me'?" he asks and then answers my question patiently. "No, you haven't said anything like that. But everything you are doing now shows a clear indication you think it is still possible to earn their love."

"Dr. Daniels, I really appreciate your insights, and you are obviously a really bright man, but that is the dumbest thing I have ever heard of-," I say dismissively, but he interrupts me again by putting up his hand.

"Sometime during your life, most likely when Maria accused you of killing your grandfather or maybe when you chose to live with your mother in the custody case, I am not really sure which, Maria and your father convinced you that you had betrayed them," he says sympathetically. "Because of this, they convinced you that you didn't deserve to be treated with love and affection."

"That doesn't-," I start to protest as Dr. Daniels raises his hand again to silence me.

"Please let me finish," Dr. Daniel says as he puts down his hand. "They convinced you that you deserved all of their abuse because of this betrayal, and if you took it, *maybe*, someday you could earn back their love."

"I really-," I start.

"David, I am not attacking you, but *if* you are ever going to get through this and the night terrors, you need to not only hear this but accept it as the truth and stop living in such a state of denial," he says calmly. "Subconsciously, you have convinced yourself that if you endure enough of their punishment, take enough of their abuse, you will prove to them that you are worthy of their love."

Dr. Daniels looks over at me, and I see he has that look in his eyes. It isn't quite the look that Alex, Matt, Patricia, and Margaret have given me over the years. Although the pity is definitely there, there is also a determination in his eyes to get me to see the truth of my situation, no matter what the cost.

"I am going to say some things that are going to upset you, but I feel you are finally ready to hear them," he says as he consults his yellow legal pad. "We all have our blind spots in life. The things we just don't see, even though they are staring us right in the face. Your blind spot is that you refuse to accept the fact that your father has never loved you and will never love you. That no matter what you do or how much abuse you take from him or Maria, in their minds, you are never going to matter to them and will always be completely expendable."

"I get it," I say sarcastically. "I am just another hooker to them. You don't need to beat me over the head with it!"

"What you are doing right now is a perfect example of what I am talking about David," Dr. Daniels says sharply.

"What?" I ask.

"All of this time you have used your sarcasm to mask your emotions, instead of actually feeling them," he says patiently. "You tell yourself, 'I am a man, I shouldn't feel this pain,' and because of that, you refuse to feel your emotions."

"Why the hell would I want to feel it?" I ask defensively.

"Until you allow yourself to experience the pain of this rejection, you will never fully acknowledge it is real," he says with an intensity in his voice I haven't heard before. "Deep down there is still a little boy inside of you that thinks he can still earn his father's love. That is why you keep falling for his deception and continue to accept his abuse."

"A little boy, give me a break!" I say defensively. "That's-"

"We are going to end our session early today," Dr. Daniels says quickly with his hand now raised again and before I can protest he says, "I want you to think about what I said, but not respond in session right now. Write down anything you want to say for our next session when you get home. Right now, I just want you to think about what I said."

Slowly I get up from the couch, but I don't want to leave. I don't want to end the session with this just hanging in the air. I start to walk out of the room and then I turn around to say just this and see Dr. Daniels scribbling furiously on the yellow legal pad.

He is just trying to help. I think to myself. *Stop trying to control everything and just leave.*

On the drive back to Sarah's that night I can't get what Dr. Daniels said out of my mind. I begin to wonder how bad the night terrors are going to be and decide to sleep in the guest bedroom.

"I think I am going to sleep in the guest bedroom tonight," I tell Sarah as we get ready for bed. "We went through some pretty intense stuff, and I don't want to scare you again."

"What did you talk about?" Sarah asks me as she pulls down the covers to our bed.

An hour later, I finish telling Sarah what happened. At this point in our relationship, I tell her everything, especially when it comes to the night terrors. We have become a team, and I try and be there for her as much as she is there for me. Every day, I try to be the best man I can be not only with her but her family as well.

"Sleep in bed with me tonight. If you get triggered, you can move to the guest bedroom," she says after I finish telling her what we talked about in session. "I am glad he is getting you to look at things for what they are, and I think that is going to really help you."

As soon as I woke up the next day, I turned to Sarah and asked, "How bad was it?" She turned toward me and smiled. "You didn't wake up once," she said as she kissed me on the cheek.

I would like to say that after that session with Doctor Daniel, I was magically healed. That I never woke up again in the middle of the night screaming for my life. Unfortunately, that just didn't happen. While I finally accepted the truth and the world became a better place for me, I would still find myself falling back on my old thinking. Deep down, I wanted him to be wrong; I wanted to mean something to my family in Texas.

Every day for the next two years, feelings of rage and hurt grew and subsided as the memories and shame flooded back. Every day for two years, I tried to deal with having my best intentions used against me, and my desire to be loved exploited by someone so cruel.

I didn't tell the family about "Johnny Russell." I simply lived my life with Sarah, while I pushed my conscience and shame down deep. Everything was playing out as my father knew it would, I was afraid of upsetting my sisters' lives; the thought of their shame in the community if Todd's double life were revealed was too much to bear.

The money simply wasn't worth it to me.

During those two years, I would frequently reach out to Pastor Landon. While I was in Los Angeles and he was in Texas, we prayed together several times over the phone. The advice and wisdom he shared helped me greatly and I will forever be in his debt.

Once the night terrors had abated, I stopped going to Dr. Daniels and tried to get on with my life. What I wouldn't admit, even to Sarah, is that I secretly hoped for, waited for, something like regret from my father. Regret that we didn't have a loving relationship. Regret that he had pulled me into such a sordid life. Regret that he chose money over his own flesh and blood.

But he had no regrets, other than that of me being born.

He doesn't think he has done anything wrong. I would think to myself late at night. *He really chose money over his own son and daughters!*

Every time a celebrity displaying the same type of behavior my father had displayed appeared in the headlines, I wondered if I made the right decision. The issues and events surrounding Bill Cosby, Charlie Sheen, and Lamar Odom all made me wonder, *did I do the right thing by walking away?*

This all changed February 17, 2015.

On that day, I received a text from Madison wishing me a happy birthday. Also, she informed me she was pregnant with a baby boy. I was going to be an uncle! My initial joy turned to panic very quickly as I realized who his grandfather would be.

Veronica's kids are two of the most important people in my life. They are the light and joy that keeps me going; there is no other way to describe them. I am blessed in the fact that my sister and brother in law are so generous in allowing me to be a regular part of their lives. I would gladly walk in front of a bus to protect them.

I knew I couldn't risk my nephew being subjected to the same type of exploitation my father had used on me.

My night terrors came back with a vengeance. I was literally leaping out of bed and terrifying Sarah. I started spending all of my nights in the guest bedroom because I was afraid I would hurt her accidentally. With no other choices left, I went back to Dr. Daniels. I wanted his professional opinion about what I should do next.

"My main concern is my nephew," I say after I catch him up on the situation. "I don't know if my sisters or anyone in the family knows about 'Johnny Russell,' with the exception of Maria."

"Maria knows?" he asks.

"We haven't talked about it, if that is what you are asking," I say. "But she is too smart not to know what is going on. He is the opposite of discreet."

"Have you had any contact with the family since your father stopped talking with you?" Dr. Daniels asks.

"No," I say. "I did take Bernard to lunch to thank him for being nice to me during my childhood when I was in Texas meeting our pastor."

"Why did you stop talking to your Texas family?" he asks calmly.

"I don't know," I say after a moment. "I guess it just didn't feel right pretending everything was alright and didn't want to lie to them."

"It goes a lot deeper than that David," he says as he consults his yellow legal pad. "I was very blunt with you in one of our last sessions about how your father and Maria really feel about you and their intentions. Do you remember what I told you?"

"I remember what you said," I say quietly.

"You knew what I told you was true, but were still holding on to some hope that your father and Maria hadn't been using you for decades to get at your inheritance," he says, and I interrupt him.

"The money isn't that big a deal," I say quickly. "I obviously let it go. I didn't sue, and it has been two and a half-"

Dr. Daniels raises his hand to stop me and continues. "The money while important isn't relevant to what I am concerned about. What is important is why *you* haven't contacted the rest of your family."

"I don't want to suck them into this mess," I say. "That isn't such a bad thing."

"No it isn't, but that isn't the only reason you haven't contacted them," Dr. Daniels says as he looks me directly in the eyes again and I cringe a little. "The real reason you haven't contacted them is you are afraid they are going to confirm that not only your father and Maria don't care about you, but the rest of the family as well. That you are expendable in their eyes too."

I start to say something and then stop. There is a huge lump in my throat, and my chest hurts a little. Once again, Dr. Daniels is right. While I had come to accept my father and Maria were sorry I was alive, I had still been holding out hope that the rest of the family cared about me.

I didn't want all of the time I spent in Texas, my entire childhood to be a lie.

"You think they will turn their backs on me too?" I ask. "What if they really don't know the truth about "Johnny Russell?"

"David, while it is a possibility that they don't know the full extent of things, I am sure they know something," he says in a resigned tone. "This level of acting out doesn't just happen and is usually the result of decades of enabling behavior by those closest to the Narcissist."

"Dr. Daniels, I am not so sure about that," I say quickly. "They really didn't know about the accident. With all of the secrets in the family, it is entirely possible that no one knows about "Johnny Russell," other than my father and Maria."

"That may be true, David," he says. "But if you are wrong or even if you are right, telling your family the truth will have serious consequences for you. The entire family will turn against you."

"I know," I say. "I have only one real question. Do you think it is possible that my father will try this type of 'bonding' with my nephew?"

"David, there are a lot of factors involved with making that type of prediction," he says a little defensively. "I haven't even sat down with your father, so there is no-"

"Taking what I told you as fact and I fully accept that you are just guessing," I say, quickly interrupting the legal mumbo jumbo. "What is your educated guess?"

Dr. Daniels sits in his chair a moment, and I can tell he is debating whether or not to tell me what he really thinks. After a couple of minutes, he finally responds.

"*If,* and it is very important that I use the word *if,* I am correct about the system of enabling that I *think* is in place in your family," he says, "then it is almost certain he will continue this type of behavior with your nephew."

"Certain?" I ask after a moment. "I thought you would say *maybe,* but not *certain*!"

"From what you described to me, your father lives in a world where there is no cost or consequence for any of his actions," he says as he starts to lecture me. "The lines of morality and even family have been erased. This environment has left your father with no moral boundaries and because of it, his acting out is getting worse over time. Now that you are out of the picture, his grandson would be his next logical choice of a family member to act out with."

"My sister would never allow him to use my nephew the w-," I say, but he interrupts me again by raising his hand.

"Your mother never knew what you and your father did when you were a child, did she?" he asks in an analytical tone. "She never knew, because your father told you not to tell her about picking up girls, the nurses, or any of the other "guy" stuff. He told you that since she wasn't a man, she wouldn't understand or maybe even get jealous. I would also *guess* that he established consequences for you sharing this information with anyone. Maybe he told you he would lose his visitation rights. Am I close in this assumption?"

"How did you know?" I ask after a moment. I am stunned, as that is exactly what happened. He even used that exact consequence.

"That's how narcissists work, David. They lie, manipulate and always put you in no-win situations so they can get what they want," he says. "They make their victims feel like they have to protect them, by telling them, 'no one else will understand them.' This type of 'emotional black-mail' and 'thought policing' is quite common in people with NPD."

"What do you think will happen if I tell everyone the truth?" I ask after a moment.

"Your father and Maria will do everything they can to discredit you within the family and eventually go after you and those closest to you," he says without hesitation.

"You think they would go after Sarah?" I ask quietly.

"Yes," he says confidently. "Why do you think he wanted to meet her?"

"I thought he wanted to see what I was doing with my life," I say quietly, as I start to think about it.

"He wanted to see what you had to lose if you stood up to him," he says sadly. "He knew you would be upset about the will. Since you lived through your ordeal, you had stopped enabling him and started standing up for what you knew was right. Your father wanted to find a new pressure point to keep you in line. Your grandmother was no longer available, so he was hoping Sarah would be her replacement. The second he saw how in love you were with Sarah, he knew you would never stand up to him and there would be no real consequences for his actions."

"But-," I manage as Dr. Daniels lands the knockout blow.

"He has been planning this since the custody battle, David." Dr. Daniels interrupts me. "A narcissist doesn't see value in people unless they enhance their image. If you threaten that image, he will go after you, the ones you love and not lose a moment's sleep while doing it. Don't make the mistake of thinking he sees you as a son."

"I hear what you are saying," I say after I take a moment to think about it. "But I have been talking with our family pastor, and he is willing to mediate something between us. I think they will see I am just trying to help-"

"David, for the past three and a half years, you have 'heard' everything," Dr. Daniels says, interrupting me again. "But you have failed to *accept* the truth of your situation. This is why I have continued to be so blunt in stating in no uncertain terms what is really happening. You need to not only hear what I am saying but completely accept it as the truth before you can get better."

"You really think my father will do this with my nephew, even after everything that has happened?" I finally ask.

"Yes," he says. "For him, it is a way to continue to establish his power and dominance over the family. Further, if you try and stop him, I think they will go after Sarah first."

"How would they even do that?" I ask.

"Suing her and going after her house," he says. "Frivolous litigation is another one of the characteristics and traits of someone with Narcissistic Personality Disorder. They know how much you love Sarah and will exploit that weakness immediately. It is just how your family dynamic works."

"Even if I involve the pastor?" I ask him after a moment. "Won't they want to look good in front of him at least?"

"They don't care anymore about what their pastor thinks than what you think. They only go to church to enhance their images," he says in a matter of fact voice. "If you challenge that carefully crafted image, they will come after you with everything they have and I want you to be prepared for it."

I did a lot of thinking after that session. For a week, my night terrors kept me in the guest bedroom as I thought about what I should do. After several long conversations with Sarah, I made my decision and my night terrors stopped that night.

March 5th, 2015 I sent my father one last text telling him in no uncertain terms I was done enabling him. We talked later that day, and he hung up on me within two minutes after threatening me.

I reached out to Pastor Landon and told him I was ready to try a spiritual intervention with my father if he was willing to help mediate a meeting with the rest of the family. I sent him a very long email listing my concerns and after talking with him, we both agreed that I should approach Maria first since my final conversation with my father resulted in him hanging up on me.

Since my father had repeatedly hung up on me in the past, I decided to communicate by email with Maria, and I was hoping and praying that Dr. Daniels was wrong with his "educated guess." I sent her an email along with the text I had sent my father detailing my concerns. I left no stone unturned with the emails and text. I wasn't going to *not* tell her the detailed truth; it was time she took responsibility for her part too.

This had gone way past a financial issue with both therapists telling me it was a safety and health issue concerning not just me, but the rest of the family.

Something I had depended on for the last two and a half years was the power of prayer.

Our Pastor instructed me to not only pray for myself and a resolution to this problem but also for the rest of my family, including my father. While I had already been praying for a resolution to this situation and the family, praying for my father was difficult. The real "Johnny" was disgusting, and the nice, accomplished "Johnny" was a fraud. How do you pray for someone who doesn't seem to have a soul?

Even though it didn't make any sense to me and I felt as if I was on a fool's errand, *I prayed for my father.*

Everything hinged on getting Maria's help. Without her, I had absolutely no chance at addressing my concerns for the family, for my nephew and myself. I knew this was an uphill battle, as she has hated me from day one. But I hoped she could see I was trying to protect my sisters and my nephew.

I knew her well enough to recognize that there wasn't any point in appealing to her sense of right and wrong. Instead, I addressed how my father's behavior created potential liabilities for the family as a whole. While I knew she didn't care for me, I also knew that appearances are everything to Maria. I thought she might be willing to help in order to protect her family's image.

Her ability to maximize any situation for her own advantage, regardless of others and regardless of what's morally right, reminds me of the characters Glenn Close plays in a lot of her films. Every single thing she says or does lacks sincerity; it's just a calculated move to push her agenda forward no matter what. She always wants to look the part of the good person, as long as it doesn't require any real sacrifice.

Actually getting her to do something good for its own sake is an uphill battle.

Getting her to even respond to an email took some doing. I was surprised that after all these years, she wasn't interested in pretending to look good anymore, let alone protecting her daughters and grandsons interests. Still, I really believed she loved my sisters. I tried to work that angle in my email to her. Maybe if she realized how exposed the girls were, she would help.

Maybe...

I sent her a second email that laid everything out. I wasn't just going to let this one go like I did when it was just a *money* issue. I tried to be firm, but sympathetic. I let her know my part in things and how I fell into the trap of enabling my father. I told her I had tried handling this on my own, but I was unable to get him to address his part in things over the years.

While I walked for the sake of the family, now that I was going to be an uncle, I simply couldn't risk leaving this unchecked. I told her I didn't want my sisters to live with the "night terrors" I had to endure, but if I couldn't find a solution to the situation, one I was comfortable with, I would have no choice but to tell them everything so they could decide for themselves what was best for them and their children.

I spilled everything, including my suspicion she had been in on this since day one. I told her my bringing this up was about making things right and making amends for enabling my father's behavior. I was cleaning up my side of the street and was willing to help her with hers.

I was done with the lying and duplicity.

I also let her know I had another step planned to make this right if they tried to sweep this under the rug, which I suspected they would. I wanted her to know this was going to get fixed one way or the other and that the next step involved more people.

This finally got her attention.

She called the next day. "First, I want to tell you I didn't know about any of this. I am going to speak about this once and then never speak about it again!" she said angrily.

I hadn't expected the call. "Can you hold on a second so I can turn off my TV?" I asked.

She hung up the phone.

I emailed her again and suggested she call someone close to her to talk about it. This was the first time I suggested Pastor Landon or her therapist. I told her helping Todd meant getting him into a 12 step program for whatever he was afflicted with, but enabling him was only hurting him and, by extension, damaging the family.

I was no longer comfortable in enabling him with my silence.

I ran through a list of all the ways my father's behavior could negatively affect the family, including his "bonding" with his new grandson, spending his daughters' inheritance on hookers and drugs, pulling his "I'm-not-paying act" on another hooker, who either kills him or has her pimp do it, or suffering a heart attack in a whorehouse and making headlines *that* way.

And those are just the measurable ways this kind of sickness can infect a family. There are a thousand smaller, more painful ways, too. For me, ignoring simply wasn't an option anymore.

The email itself was three pages long. Again, I mentioned Pastor Landon as someone we should go to for guidance in this matter.

She called me one more time. Again, I asked her if I could turn down the TV.

"I have read your emails," she replied. "Now you are just going to have to listen to me!" I told her I was happy to listen, but I wasn't going to be bulldozed on the phone.

She hung up.

I sent another email. I called several times but got no response. She was using my father's "ignore it and it will go away" tactic. When "Johnny" decided not to pay Cindy in Vegas, contrary to what she told me, Soon didn't make it right. After that, I got a flurry of angry texts and phone calls from both Soon and Cindy about my brother "Johnny." I called my father up and asked him to handle it, but he said, "Just ignore them. It's my experience that they will go away."

How many times has he done this before? I wondered as he was so casual about it.

I gave Maria a month to process the "new" information and then emailed her again. *I was done being ignored.* I knew she hadn't talked to Pastor Landon, but I referred my good Christian stepmother to Exodus 34:6-7 and again suggested that she talk with Pastor Landon. This section of the Old Testament specifically deals with the sins of the father being attached to the souls of his children. She continued to ignore me.

Finally, I told her that I had contacted Pastor Landon.

The next day, I got a very angry message from Maria telling me she had spoken with the Pastor and was removing herself from the situation. She felt she had no part in it. She was also furious I had been praying with our Pastor two and a half years for a spiritual solution to this problem and for the family. I can only assume she wanted to be the first one to spin the situation, assuring him that I was "angry" or "greedy." I couldn't believe she wasn't even going to help me try and protect the girls, after all of the things I pointed out in the emails.

Further, she told me that she had told the girls.

I hadn't planned on telling my sisters anything until after Madison had given birth, and only then if I couldn't work things out in some other way. Telling the girls was her version of circling the wagons and shutting me out, which I expected.

What Maria didn't realize was I wasn't going to let this one go; I refused to let my father treat my sisters and me like the prostitutes he took so much pleasure hurting over the years.

With no real choices left, I emailed my sisters. I told them I was sorry that they found out the truth this way about who our father was, but I had tried everything to stop it from coming out like this. I forwarded to them the emails I had sent proving my efforts (and how I still wanted to get him help but had to put a stop to his behavior), along with the first chapter of this book.

I never heard back. *Not a thing.*

Pastor Landon emailed me a couple of days later to say that he had talked with the entire family and didn't believe he could mediate in any way. I looked at all of the emails and texts, over 65 pages of my detailed thoughts and concerns about my father's issues.

In those 65 pages, I tried everything I could think of to get them to at least talk about it. My worst fears were realized when the pastor emailed me that day. After all these years, I was out of the family. I had done all I could, but I had to face it: I had no more value to them than a low-rent prostitute.

"Ignore him and he will go away."

CHAPTER FOURTEEN

THE LAST MALE DAVIS

I thought a lot about what I wanted to say in this last chapter. This is a book I really, REALLY didn't want to write and did everything I could to avoid it. When it was just a money thing, I walked away. I was afraid of what I might find if I pushed things and kept asking questions. The money just wasn't worth it to me, and I thought my sisters were covered.

When my nephew was born, everything changed. The more I pushed, the more questions I asked, the more horrified I became at the system of enabling that has helped protect Johnny Russell. I realized that I could no longer enable him with my silence and that I can't take the chance of history repeating itself.

Before writing the book, I made one last visit to Dr. Daniels. I had made my decision, but I wanted to talk with him about it. Along with our family pastor, I have to give him credit for giving me some sage advice and thank him for not pulling his punches. He got me to finally see the truth.

"Not only did they refuse to sit down with the Pastor," I tell him sadly. "But the rest of the family instantly cut off all communications with me, the second I started to talk about my concerns. I have printed out my emails to them for you to look at."

As I try to hand the printed emails to Dr. Daniels, he simply raises his hand signifying that it wasn't necessary for him to read them.

"I am sure the emails are as clear and concise as you have been in our sessions," Dr. Daniels says kindly. "Did you really expect a different reaction?"

"I guess not," I say weakly, but the truth was I had really hoped for at least some type of regret or concern over what had happened. "I guess this settles any questions I had about how they really feel about me. Doesn't it?"

"Throughout our sessions and this experience with your father and his family, I have seen you go through what is known as *the five stages of grief*," he says in that analytical tone that I have become all too familiar with. "Are you aware of Doctor Elizabeth Kubler-Ross or maybe her book *On Death and Dying*?"

"No," I say. "But I don't really see what dying has to do with anything."

"When someone experiences the death of a loved one, they normally go through five different stages of grief." Dr. Daniels tells me patiently as if he didn't even hear me. "The first stage is usually, but not always, denial and isolation."

"Are you saying I was in denial because my grandma died?" I ask.

"No. The death I am referring to is the death of the fictional relationship with your Texas family and your role in it as a son. You have been grieving the loss of something you never really had, but it feels real to you because you were so desperate to believe they loved you as a son and brother," he says, and then he sees me wince and asks, "would you like to take a moment to digest what I just said or discuss it?"

"No," I say quickly. "Please continue."

"Alright," he says as he looks down at his legal pad. "The second your father first approached you to be his *'beard/brother/cleaner'*, you immediately went into a state of denial and began to isolate yourself from the people in your life. Correct?"

"Yes, but I was trying to figure out what was wrong with him," I say defensively.

"Bargaining is another one of the five phases. It happens to be the phase that you went into next," he says sadly. "You didn't want your father to be using you, so you tried to find another answer. In essence, you started to bargain with yourself. You asked yourself things like, *'Maybe there is something wrong with my father that I can help him with?'* As time went on and you saw the depth of his depravity you continued to bargain by telling yourself, *'He has to love me. I am the last male Davis. There must be something I am missing.'* As the truth became even more self-evident, you began to convince yourself that *'I am protecting my family from the truth.'*"

"There could have been something else wrong with him. Sex addiction, drug addiction, something," I say angrily. "How was I supposed to know this was a setup? I still believe my grandmother would have died if she found out what he was doing!"

"I am not blaming you or trying to find fault with your intentions. I am simply telling you there is a clinical pattern of your behavior," he says patiently. "I know you were trying to do the right thing, but *I* am trying to get you to see that pattern. May I continue?"

"Yes," I say quickly. "Sorry, I know you are trying to help. It just-"

"It is quite alright, David. I know this is painful for you," he says sympathetically. "The next phase was anger. You experienced this when you introduced your father to Sarah. You had done everything any father could have asked for. You believed you were finally worthy of his love and had worked so hard for it. You achieved professional success, financial success, found a woman who loved you and were living a good life."

"That's-," I say, but he raises his hand.

"Please let me finish, David," he says patiently. "Instead of earning your father's love, he continued to treat you like the prostitutes he frequents and confirmed every suspicion you had about him. That is when you went into the next stage, depression."

"OK, now you are just wrong," I say angrily. "Anger I get, but I was the opposite of depressed at that time."

"Depression manifests itself in different ways, and you don't always see it," Dr. Daniels says but sees the face I am making and shakes his head. "Not all depression is rooted in feeling sad. This depression manifested itself in two ways. The practical side, which was you trying to protect your sisters and your inheritance from "Johnny Russell," and the second was more subtle, subconsciously preparing yourself for when your family inevitably turns their backs on you. Whether you want to call it depression or not is up to you, but it can be clinically diagnosed as a form of depression."

"I-," I start to interrupt again but stop myself before he can raise his hand. Everything he is saying is once again, 100% right on the money. I feel strange because I feel the first bit of relief that I have felt in a long time now by sharing this with him.

"The final stage is acceptance," he continues. "That is where you are at now, as you have finally confirmed all of your worst fears. Those things you so often joked about as a way to avoid feeling the actual pain of their rejection have finally come to fruition. Now you can finally accept that you mean nothing to them and are standing up against that rejection."

"Are you saying the book is a bad idea?" I ask.

"No, far from it, but I doubt you would listen to me if I said it was," he says after a moment's thought. "You are standing up for what you know in your heart is right. What you think will ultimately protect your family from your father's alter ego. What I hope is that at some point you protect the one person who hasn't had an advocate in all of this."

"My nephew?" I ask.

"No David. You," he says as he looks up from his legal pad and right at me. "In all of our sessions you have talked about protecting everyone but yourself. This stems from the fact that you have been raised to believe that it is selfish to think of yourself and your own self-interests. In essence, that it is selfish to protect yourself."

"But isn't that what my father does?" I ask. "Only think of himself and his self-interests?"

"He does it in the most extreme terms." Dr. Daniels sighs as he says, "he sees only what benefits him and no one else. Because you are a good person, you have looked at his example and done the exact opposite. I can only assume that while you were growing up, you saw your grandmother as the only good example in the family and followed her example a little too closely."

"Too closely? I could do a lot worse than being like my grandmother," I say defensively. "Not that I come close to being that good of a person. She-"

"There is no doubt your grandmother was an amazing woman," he says quickly, cutting me off. "You definitely imprinted on her for that reason, but too much of anything can be a bad thing. You have been conditioned to always turn the other cheek and walk away when it comes to family conflict. Because of this, you have failed to stand up for yourself and what is right for you."

"Is that so bad?" I say. "I was just trying to protect them from them the truth."

"I know, David, and the book may end up stopping the cycle of abuse that not only you but everyone else who comes into contact with 'Johnny Russell' suffers," he says with a great deal of compassion in his voice. "It is just my hope that one day, you will realize that there is no stigma attached to standing up for yourself, as well as others. That you realize that you deserve to be treated with the same dignity, love, respect and kindness as everyone else deserves in a family environment."

"I understand that already," I say after a moment. "My time with Sarah taught me that much."

"I believe it has, David," he says with a very satisfied tone in his voice as he looks down at his legal pad and then back up at me. "For the first time in all of our sessions, I believe you not only have heard me but are finally accepted what I am telling you as the truth."

At that moment, the timer went off. I realized our time was done in more than one way. In finally accepting the truth for what it is and not for what I wanted it to be, I was now ready to set things right.

As I started writing the book, putting it down on paper, things became even clearer to me. When you stare at something in black and white, there is no real way to hide from the truth. In writing down each action, I painted a crystal clear picture of not only what happened, but of my father and Maria's ultimate agenda.

The sad truth is that my father and Maria would have been much happier if I had died on the road that day. I had no more value to them than that of a used printer cartridge. To them I was something to be discarded after use.

Further, my father didn't view just me, but everyone he came into contact with that way and that frightened me.

How long until he starts using my nephew to convince some random women in the park that she is safe with him? I wondered. *Would he leave my nephew's stroller with her friends, as they go off somewhere?*

While this may sound farfetched to some, I need only look back at my childhood to validate this very real fear. I had seen enough of "Johnny Russell," to know that anything was possible at this point. The more I wrote, the more convinced I became that I was doing the right thing. During this time, my mother told me the story of when my father challenged their custody agreement.

She was shocked that he wanted custody and tried to reason with him.

"Why are you doing this? You haven't shown any interest in him before, and you get to see him on holidays. You are single and don't have the time it would take to raise him right now," she said to him. "I am a great mother and put in the time with him that he needs. The court is going to see that this just isn't right."

"Right or wrong doesn't matter in court," he shot back at her. "I have money, and you don't. I can afford the best lawyers money can buy, and you can barely afford to pay your rent. If you fight me on this, you will lose, and I will make sure you never see David again."

I realized when she was telling me this story that my father has always been "Johnny Russell." The only thing that has changed over time is that he has gotten better at hiding it. While I am no expert (I am not a physician or in any way trained to render a professional opinion), as a son I can also safely say that I think my father needs help, and there are resources available to him.

The Texas State Medical Board has a program called The Physicians Health Program which assists doctors with addiction and psychological issues. It is made up of a board of fellow physicians that independently verify and monitor a doctor's progress in recovery. Sadly, I don't believe a therapist of "his" choosing is going to help him at this point.

I believe the only hope he has is someone who is not on the payroll and who can hold him accountable for his actions.

As for my suspicions he has been inappropriately prescribing medication to himself and others, The Texas State Medical Board can do a simple check of his DEA registration number and that will clear that question up in about ten seconds. If he is willing to get honest with himself and others, I am sure the DEA diversion control office that handles such information will take that into account.

For what it is worth, I hope I am wrong, but everything I have seen indicates my father has some major problems that represent a health risk not just for himself, but others as well.

"Can't you just be happy your life is going so well in Los Angeles and not cause problems?" was one of the last things Maria asked me after the blow up at my grandmother's house. I didn't answer her then, but I have the answer now. "No, I can't. I can't be happy until I stop pretending what happened didn't happen, and I'm sure no one else will suffer the way I did."

By writing this book, I am starting to redraw the lines of basic human decency for my father. If I don't, it is simply a matter of time until he does it again. Sadly, I am somewhat relieved that Maria didn't agree to help me make things right. Her tendency to re-write history would always have me wondering exactly which version of the truth she was telling. In the digital age, a book is something that you can't sweep under the rug or deny.

A book is a written record of everything that has happened and it functions as a warning to others to not fall into the same trap I did.

As the "last male Davis" in our line, I have two responsibilities that I can no longer ignore. The first is telling the truth no matter what that might cost me and the second is doing everything I can to protect my nephew and sisters. Even though my sisters have rejected me, I still love them and feel an obligation as their brother to protect them and my nephew as I try to make things right.

It doesn't take an expert to figure out my "night terrors" are my conscience reminding me I can't just walk away.

When I realize the depth of the enabling and denial surrounding this situation, I came up with ten steps that I was willing to take to not only protect my sisters and nephew but also to make amends for my part in things as well. At that time, I naively thought I would never have to go past step three; my denial still ran that deep. We are now on step six of this journey of redemption, as listed below:

Step 1 - Confront father.

Step 2 - Seek spiritual counseling.

Step 3 - Tell Maria and getting into spiritual counseling with family.

Step 4 - Write book.

Step 5 - Send family book.

Step 6 - Publish book.

After everything I have seen now, I think it will be step 8 or 9 before they finally see the light in this situation. "Ignore it and it will go away" is simply not an option for me. My purpose in coming back from my accident is clear to me now. It was time for me to tell the truth and fix this to ensure it doesn't happen again.

Having crossed over to the other side, I was given a glimpse into a world where material desires play no part in people's actions. Everything in that world centered on the shared experience, community and love. A place where everyone felt like family and there was no greed or inequality. I realize now our life here is simply a snapshot of who we really are, with our actions and word being the only thing we take with us on our journey.

While we are in this moment in time, the choices we make stay with us forever. Each step we take is a test to see if we are worthy enough to ascend. God gave me the ability to make this right, to stand up for not only my sisters and my nephew, but finally, stand up for myself as well. This is not only a moral but spiritual journey for me to save not only my sisters and nephews souls but mine as well.

We have been put on this planet to learn certain lessons. I have been given a second chance to tell the truth and make things right. To make sure this never happens again and to stand up against my father's belief that money and power somehow exclude him from his moral responsibilities as a father, grandfather, doctor and human being.

Knowing that my father and Maria will take their actions with them from this world, I almost feel pity for them at this point. I say almost because I am only human, and I want to be as honest as I can be with this book. I have forgiven them their trespasses against me, not because I believe they are repentant, but because I longer wish to be a victim, and no longer wish to carry that brick in my backpack.

There is too much I want to do with the second chance I have been given.

I want to build a family of my own where kindness and discipline are practiced. I want to be a man who is the exact opposite of my biological father: I will build my children up, not tear them down. But to start that life, I still have one obligation left as the last male Davis; I have to fix this.

I have to break the cycle.

The truth is I will never know the formal diagnosis for my father. But I don't care if he's a sex addict, who won't seek help. I don't even care if he's a narcissist or a textbook psychopath. It is my job to see that the destructive cycles are broken, innocent people are protected and that the truth, however painful, be known.

Not once did my father or Maria ask how they might make things right. Not once did they acknowledge that the games he played with prostitutes are a disgusting and degrading form of personal entertainment; they never even acknowledged that it's illegal, much less morally abhorrent. They thought their jobs, education, social status and money put them above any real consequences.

One of the things I wanted to bring to the table in spiritual counseling with my family was establishing The Wanda Davis Foundation (Wdavisfoundation.com).

The WDF would have been an organization that would help women who want to escape the world of prostitution and transition back into a regular life. The organization would aid in everything from substance abuse issues, transitional housing, continued education and counseling for emotional issues as well as giving them a safe place to live while they built a new life.

I saw taking this action as a way to give a voice to those my father has taken advantage of all of his life and a way to build a better life for those less fortunate than him.

I was hoping this idea would bring the family together somehow and start to make amends for our father's actions. We would be reversing the cycle of abuse as a family. After our pastor let me know that they were not interested in even talking about what happened, I knew I was alone in my journey to make this one right.

I realize now that real sacrifice, restitution, and remorse are things my father and Maria will try to avoid at every turn. They would rather paint over the situation or talk around it, instead of taking action. I can only thank God that I am not like them and hope my actions will demonstrate that fact.

Twenty percent of all of the money I make from this book will go to establishing and funding The Wanda Davis Foundation. In purchasing this book, you have already made a contribution.

The offer I was hoping to make my sisters still stands; if they want to help make this right, I will welcome their involvement. I would actually donate more, but I don't know if I am ever going to work again after publishing this book.

It's not exactly something you put on a resume.

In taking this action, I have given up any chance of inheriting what my grandmother left me, given up any chance to have a relationship with my Texas family, and I know they will come after me. I don't take the step I am about to take lightly, but if it keeps my nephew or any other member of my family from ever meeting "Johnny Russell," in person, it is a small price to pay.

I'll chalk it up as another part of my penance.

I went to my grandmother's grave site several times over the years to pray for answers and guidance on what to do next. I kept on coming back to the same thought: *if she had known everything, the one thing she would have done was protect the child at all costs.*

For years, that's what she did with me.

In taking this action, I am not only rejecting how my father values me and the rest of his family but most importantly his core values. He has put the entire family in a no-win situation to get what he wants, and someone has to stop this cycle of abuse and manipulation.

Once the cycle is broken, I will finally be able to put this behind me.

Until then, I will continue to appreciate and enjoy the most precious gift I have been given in all of this, *my life*. Every day I thank God for all of the gifts I have been given in life and allowing me to enjoy the journey.

In accepting things for what they are, instead of what I wanted them to be, I have started to take the bricks out of my backpack and no longer have to carry the weight of my father's actions on my soul.

The Abortionist's Son is a title I came up with when I was angry, and I couldn't really think of a more appropriate one. The truth is that I am the one abortion my father now wishes he could have performed...

I accept that now, but it no longer has any power over me.

...TELLING THE TRUTH WOULD
COST YOU YOUR FAMILY

www.ingramcontent.com/pod-product-compliance
Lightning Source LLC
La Vergne TN
LVHW011321080426
835513LV00006B/146